Evolutionary Basic Democracy

DOI: 10.1057/9781137338662

The Theories, Concepts and Practices of Democracy

General Editor: **Jean-Paul Gagnon**, School of Political Science and International Studies and the School of Mathematics and Physics, University of Queensland, Australia

The discourse of democracy suffers from ambiguity: its literature is too vast and there is no codified understanding of its theories, concepts and practices. The uncertainties surrounding the meaning of democracy resulted in serious political problems for all levels of democratic government – both historically and presently. The literature on democracy is so vast that it is highly improbable for one person to understand the core of this mass. Such an understanding is, however, needed to resolve the problematic ambiguity associated with democracy.

The aim of this book series is to define, analyse and organize democracy's hundreds of theories, concepts and practices. The objectives, supporting this aim, are as follows:

- Curate and consider works on democracy;
- Identify and fill gaps in the literature on historical and contemporary democracies;
- Find opportunities to synthesize or separate specific theories, concepts or practices of democracy.

Titles include:

Mark Chou
THEORISING DEMOCIDE
Why and How Democracies Fail

Ramin Jahanbegloo
DEMOCRACY IN IRAN

Jean-Paul Gagnon
EVOLUTIONARY BASIC DEMOCRACY
A Critical Overture

The Theories, Concepts and Practices of Democracy
Series Standing Order ISBN 978-1-137-29817-1
(*outside North America only*)

You can receive future titles in this series as they are published by placing a standing order. Please contact your bookseller or, in case of difficulty, write to us at the address below with your name and address, the title of the series and the ISBN quoted above.

Customer Services Department, Macmillan Distribution Ltd, Houndmills, Basingstoke, Hampshire RG21 6XS, England

palgrave▸pivot

Evolutionary Basic Democracy: A Critical Overture

Jean-Paul Gagnon

Research Fellow, School of Political Science and International Studies, University of Queensland

palgrave
macmillan

DOI: 10.1057/9781137338662

First published 2013 by
PALGRAVE MACMILLAN

Palgrave Macmillan in the UK is an imprint of Macmillan Publishers Limited, registered in England, company number 785998, of Houndmills, Basingstoke, Hampshire RG21 6XS.

Palgrave Macmillan in the US is a division of St Martin's Press LLC, 175 Fifth Avenue, New York, NY 10010.

Palgrave Macmillan is the global academic imprint of the above companies and has companies and representatives throughout the world.

Palgrave® and Macmillan® are registered trademarks in the United States, the United Kingdom, Europe and other countries

ISBN: 978-1-137-33867-9 EPUB
ISBN: 978-1-137-33866-2 PDF
ISBN: 978-1-137-33865-5 Hardback

This book is printed on paper suitable for recycling and made from fully managed and sustained forest sources. Logging, pulping and manufacturing processes are expected to conform to the environmental regulations of the country of origin.

A catalogue record for this book is available from the British Library.

A catalog record for this book is available from the Library of Congress.

www.palgrave.com/pivot

DOI: 10.1057/9781137338662

To John Keane for heartening my confidence

Contents

DOI: 10.1057/9781137338662

List of Tables and Figures

Tables

Figure

Preface

It would be helpful to state three things in this Preface. The first is the concept of democracy that I use in this book. The second is the working status of the model I present in the book's Introduction. And the third concerns the way this book fulfils its promises.

The definition of democracy that I use comes from my journal article entitled 'Democratic Theory and Theoretical Physics', which was published by the *Taiwan Journal of Democracy* (a robust and open-access academic periodical). For that paper I collected works that together explained more than 40 different types of democracy. And, using computational analytics, I asked that body of data what these different types of democracy had in common. This work resulted in the first argument for the theory of basic democracy. At that point I thought that for any democracy to exist, the polity or society in question has to have an observable engagement with the following six parameters:

1) a non-violent citizenry;
2) the citizenry declaring and exercising its sovereignty;
3) a discourse on equality;
4) communication on social, political, economic and similar topics;
5) a process of collectively deciding leadership;
6) and a means to collectively determine, and then pursue, a society's long-term goals.

A particular style of democracy emerges depending on the way a polity or society engages the parameters above. The

DOI: 10.1057/9781137338662

emergent style depends on what problems exist in these engagements, what institutions have been built and what normative communal desires exist about each parameter.

This is the way that I understand democracy and discuss it from Chapters 1 to 4. It is the lens that I use to look at nonhumans. That being said, my definition is inescapably subjective and parochial. If a different scholar deployed my analytical study it is possible that she would build a different list from my own. Also, when I revisited my paper to add more types of democracy to my analyses, I noticed that the vast majority of democracy types that I originally used were Eurocentric. They were also bound to specific *times* in a mostly Eurocentric history. Because of that, this theory of mine is limited and cannot speak for the world. It does not represent 'democracy itself' but rather a conception of what a specific type of democracy might be. Every theory of democracy suffers the same.

The problems raised in my conceptual work resulted in the model of democracy that I offer in the Introduction. I am building this model at the University of Queensland. It is a real and existing project. The model is in the process of being designed for 4-dimensional use on the Internet. My aim is to establish and then manage a collaborative research programme designed to populate the model with data on democracy. These data must come from all known planetary space and all known human *and* nonhuman time. We will need to bring in these data from as many languages as possible. As I explain in greater detail below, we need this body of carefully organized data to reach a scientific definition of democracy. Without a definition of this type – something that must be widely agreed upon by scientists and philosophers alike – we cannot with certainty say what is democratic and what is not. This is one root of certain serious problems in the contemporary politics of the world.

The American philosopher Sidney Hook said it best in his 1949 work 'The Philosophy of Democracy as a Philosophy of History' (p. 582):

> The recognition that our own lives and those of our descendants depend mainly upon the political decisions we take in this generation makes political ideas today causal factors of the first rank. It reinforces the necessity for an analysis of the democratic ideals that are invoked as principles of justification. It is at this point particularly that philosophers can do a much needed work of clarification. One of the most curious phenomena of our time is the way in which all totalitarian governments have sought to pass themselves off as species of democracy – as 'organic democracies,' 'directed

DOI: 10.1057/9781137338662

> democracies,' 'higher democracies.' And it is intellectually scandalous that even some American philosophers have lent themselves to this campaign of semantic corruption which judges a culture not by its practices and institutions but by the holiday rhetoric with which its public documents and officials gloss them over. Such stupendous naiveté which would make every ruthless despot a brother democrat provided he talks about the classless society, or about the brotherhood of man under the fatherhood of God, is a preface to political folly.

Hook's point reveals the seriousness of the predicament we are in concerning democracy's condition of problematic uncertainty. Part of my book's purpose is to detail a method that will resolve this global political issue.

My book is an introduction. It is an *overture* to a different way of thinking about democracy. It is meant to set the grounds for further research. Because of that, the book is meant to be capacious. It has to raise more questions than it answers. The book fosters the growth of what I think is an already established, but rather new, ontology of democracy.

DOI: 10.1057/9781137338662

Acknowledgements

This book is technically my third contracted book for Palgrave Macmillan, but the first of the three to be published. It (the book being an entity unto its own now) and I owe a great deal to two specific individuals at Palgrave Macmillan: Amber Stone-Galilee, senior editor for politics, and Andrew Baird, editorial assistant for politics. From letter of inquiry to final manuscript submission my work was put under impressive editorial scrutiny. It was sent for blind peer-review multiple times and fit to the format that would best suit the book's chances on the market. Communication was efficient. The editors worked hard to answer every one of my enquiries. I am grateful to you both for your kindness and professionalism. My thanks also go to Newgen Knowledge Works.

As the book was in its final drafts, I sent individual chapters to colleagues asking for candid appraisals. Dr Mark Chou, Phil Paine, Dr Ron Levy, Professor Steven Muhlberger and Professor Gavin Kendall contributed generously. Their critical remarks were poignant and were of great value.

Chapter 2 of this book is indebted to a number of brilliant minds that agreed to share their time with me. I am grateful to Professor Uwe Meierhenrich for discussing the notion of democratic prebiotic and amino acid behaviour, Professor Zhi-zhong Xing for explaining how quarks and leptons can be made democratic, Dr Austin Lund for deconstructing a baker's dozen of physics papers to me specifying how and why 'democracy' and 'democratic' were used therein, Associate Professor Tamara Davis for answering my weird questions on 'democracy in outer space', Professor Kevin Foster for explaining the uncertainties biologists have about gamete social behaviour, Dr Darryl Preece for easily explaining 4-dimensionality to me (he deserves a prize for his teaching skills) and Professor Gerard Milburn for setting me on the right path of inquiry.

I would like to thank Sarah Chen for her professionalism, artistry and enthusiasm. She brought the model of evolutionary basic democracy to visual-life for which I am interminably grateful. To others who follow the siren call of social and political philosophy (or theory) and would like to employ visualisation in their works, please think of Sarah Chen: scientific illustrator extraordinaire at http://www.sarahachen.com/.

It is to a specific ten-year old boy, and nephew, named Max that I would like to express my gratitude. One day after school I showed him the table of animate nonhuman democracies (Table 1.1). I had just finished reading a large number of papers on microbial cooperation and was excited about this burgeoning field. Max asked whether the table was about species making decisions with *other* species. This was a subtle dimension of the literature, one that I did not think to pursue. This led to the paragraph on interspecies democracy in Chapter 2. Thanks to you Max for your poignant question. I hope that you continue to nurture your curiosity and to ask the questions that need asking.

I owe a special debt to the University of Queensland, specifically the School of Political Science and International Studies as well as the School of Mathematics and Physics for their support. Without these institutional pillars the writing of this book would not have been possible. Great thanks go specifically to Dr Martin Weber, Professor Gillian Whitehouse, Professor Halina Rubinstein-Dunlop, Associate Professor Richard Devetak, Dr Heloise Weber, Professor Stephen Bell, Professor Jean-Louis Durand, Dr Phil Orchard, Dr Shannon Brincat, Dr Frank Mols, Professor Roland Bleiker, Dr Ian Ward, Dr Sebastian Kaempf and Kamil Shah.

Finally, I want to thank my family, friends and the strangers that I have yet to make friends of, for their unexpectedly courageous support, unyielding encouragement and uncompromising generosity. These thanks go especially to my beautiful wife Tracey – the greatest of my muses. I take full responsibility for any flaws in this book. I would, however, like to share the success its strong points might enjoy with all thanked above and the many others who are too numerous to mention.

Introduction: A New Analytic Tool

Abstract: *This introduction offers a post-foundational analytic tool for the study of democracy across time and space. The tool helps to manage the complexity of the discourse on democracy. This chapter argues that we do not know what democracy is. The chapter is determined to offer a way forward. It establishes that this book will explain a theory of basic democracy. It describes that the democracy theories, concepts, practices and their nuances are many and that the resulting ambiguity interferes with politics globally. The lack of a scientific definition of democracy is a serious and present danger for contemporary politics and society. This logic is used to argue for the importance of the model and to justify why we need a way forward.*

Gagnon, Jean-Paul. *Evolutionary Basic Democracy: A Critical Overture*, Basingstoke: Palgrave Macmillan, 2013. DOI: 10.1057/9781137338662.

Apparently there are many democracies today. Some places are not democratic. Certain democracies are more democratic and others less. We are told that everyone wants democracy and that everyone is a democrat. Individuals tell themselves that this is what they want. Democracy is the end of one history and the beginning of another. It is a crowning human achievement or a failing utopia. Some say it existed for a long time. Others say that it has still yet to arrive. Local, local-regional, national, federal, international, multinational, and global politics *as well as* societies are driven by the desire to have democracy or to be democratic.

There is, however, a troubling difficulty with the statements I make above. We do not know what democracy is. We do not know what it means, or where it came from, or where it is going. It is universally pervasive in politics and society but, at the same time, an empty and confusing *thing*. Classicists debate the origins of the word. They debate the meaning ancient Greeks intended for it. They argue that the Greek were defining something already in existence. Democracy was not invented by the Greek. Its institutions across time and space are contradictory. Its theory is unimaginably complicated. Madness has gripped us. If democracy is everywhere and everyone wants it, then how do we not know what it means? If we do not know what democracy means, then why is it forcefully driving our politics and societies? Humanity is governed by whispers and ghosts, by smoke and shadows that change from ear to ear, eye to eye, and thought to thought. It is imprisoned by parochialism, subjectivity, and myopia. Democracy means nothing. It means everything. We are in trouble.

This book's sole purpose is to *introduce* a descriptive and analytical tool that will eventually permit us to understand democracy *for the first time*. It is a passage to a new ontology. The book presents a model. It then reverse engineers this model to describe a theory. This theory thinks about democracy across time and space. It breaks out of anthropocentric bonds. It explores nonhumans and inanimate matter. It demands a scientific foundation for democracy. A foundation that is reproducible by others and that is based on data from every corner of the earth and all of human time. We have to take everything that we think is democracy or democratic from every language and then ask this gargantuan body the same questions, over and over: What are you? How do you work? Where do you come from? And where can you take us? This book is designed to alter politics and society because it allows us to ask and answer these

DOI: 10.1057/9781137338662

questions. Democracy can be defined. But it must be done in a way unlike any other before it.

We need to think about democracy differently. In its current form across a number of languages the only certainty (Dunn, 2013) is that the word itself – *mínzhŭ*, *δημοκρατία*, *democrat/c/zie/a*, *демократия* – has existed for some time. We are capable of tracking the word across specific times and spaces even though the historical record is far patchier than some are ready to admit. The word has been used to describe many forms of government, governance and institutions.

The definition of democracy is, and has been, contested (Gallie, 1956) since its North African, Mesoasiatic, Grecian, or other etymological births. Although the Greek word δημοκρατία is presently the norm to designate what we think is democracy and democratic, this does not need to be the case. There are earlier languages pre-dating Herodotus or Cleisthenes which had a lexicon referring to practices that are today considered democratic (Isakhan, 2012: 8). The political theorist John Keane (2009) argued this to be undeniably apparent in Mycenaean Linear B script. The French philosopher Yves Schemeil (2000) also argued this point during the construction of his archaeopolitics[1] concept. It is likely that more evidence will emerge from the study of non-elite society and language by Egyptologists (McDowell, 1999; Meskell, 1998; and Ambridge, 2007), the increasing focus in archaeology and historical anthropology on ancient pastoral or nomadic societies (Tebes, 2007; Lewis, 1999 [1961]) and research into other parts of the world during the contemporaneous times of democratic Hellas. An example for the latter comes from a French work by Memel-Fotê (1991: 270):

> Contemporary democratic theorists identify one essential characteristic for any democracy to exist: that is the institutionalised participation of a people regarding public life. There are five actions within this participation. (1) Taking one's part in the assembly, (2) engaging in dialogue, (3) participating in decision-making, (4) playing a role in the execution of the decision or participating in the specification of how a decision is to be executed, and (5) sharing or having control over the entire process. In the first case, there are villages [in Africa] where the people decide who is to be their first among equals [leader]. This decision is made consensually taking into account the person's societal pre-eminence including their material resources and intellectual capacities. The latter is observable in certain pre-colonial rural societies within Cote d'Ivoire and certain pygmy hunter-gatherer societies. In the second case, 'all decide all' in an assembly of children, adults, and the aged with one unique characteristic: the wielding of power is bound by

> a rotation resembling one described in Aristotle's typologies. This is a practice found within the age-class systems of the *Ebrie* hunter-agriculturalists (Cote d'Ivoire) and *Gykuyu* agriculturalists (Kenya) [translated from the original in French].

The point above can be extended to places in the Russian Far East and mainland south-east Asia (present day Vietnam, Laos, southern China, Cambodia) where certain indigenous minorities have inclusive, egalitarian societies that are explainable in the ways that Memel-Fotê used for pre-colonial Nubian Africa. The description of any democracy, even those contemporaneous to ancient Hellas and including ancient Hellas, will be subjective and open to a diversity of 'democracy interpretations'. This is in part due to a lack of a positivist[2] definition of democracy that is able to explain its raw, human essence.

The contestation of democracy as a concept is a topic in the political philosophies of thinkers like Aristotle and Plato. The theory of democracy's worth and its practicality has been long debated. But the ethos of the practice itself does not have this attention even though it differs from place to place. Ancient Athens, Sparta, Chaonia, and villages bordering the coast of the Levant, North Africa, Europe and the Black Sea had differing democratic ethoi and institutions. Classicists like Asmonti (2006), Pritchard (2010) and Sissa (2012) elucidate the nuances of ancient democracy from conception to practice. There is a heterogeneity of historical democracies that the literature is focusing on. In previous centuries, books or papers describing the delicate ethos or telos of a particular archaic democracy were rare. It appears today, as works of that sort continue to be published, that this trend is thankfully changing.

The bulk of the evidence I provide in the paragraphs above is not widely known. What is less known is that we do not know what democracy is. Types, theories, concepts, and practices of democracy as well as their many nuances are certainly known. Some of them are well-represented by the literature. A number of them are well-described. But due to the sheer scale of the literature on democracy it is improbable to know them all. This complex body of democracies leads and has led to experimental research, growth in philosophy, and innovative practical morphologies across the globe. But democracy itself, that raw essence shared between the hundreds of different democracies known to us, is still an unknown variable.

This state of affairs erodes the meaning of democracy. Its disturbance confounds the discourse and contemporary political practice of democracy as everything we think to be democracy in this sense cannot be. We

DOI: 10.1057/9781137338662

do not know what democracy is so how can we determine what its many variations are? At the same time however this fact also provides an avenue to answering, through a positivist definition, what this raw essence is. Even without knowing democracy's first order definition, we can still use the term to different effects and certainly use the data available to us to uncover its raw essence. This is something we will turn to shortly.

For now, the word 'democracy' is currently associated with hundreds of 'democracy' manifestations across numerous literatures (see Held, 2006; Gagnon, 2010, for more). We attach it to systems of government or governance that are at times fundamentally at odds with each other. A look at some of the arguments between assembly and representative (Kornblith and Jawahar, 2005; Urbinati, 2010) or liberal and radical (Hamington, 2004; Selg, 2012; Wingenbach, 2011) democratic theories is indicative of this condition in the discourse.

There are proponents in the literature that maintain this uncertainty over the origins of democracy to be a boon. It is true that a given amount of uncertainty about the positivist definition of anything is useful. This allows us to issue challenges which might invariably improve the definition. Keane says this about the physicist Werner Heisenberg's work in the late 1920s on uncertainty and how social science can benefit from Heisenberg's principle. So too does Wingenbach (2011) at the beginning of his work on institutionalizing agonistic democracy. But too much uncertainty can obfuscate a definition to the point of eroding meaning. Democracy, for example, was contested since the Greeks developed the term to describe an already existing social and political set of phenomena. Democracy was contested in the early days of the Cold War between the USA and the USSR. It is contested today by numerous countries that are labelled undemocratic and by the demoi of countries that are themselves labelled democratic.

In sum, the global epistemology of democracy is out of control. No one person can understand the vast complexity of this literature – of its hundreds of nuances across multiple languages. It is seemingly going everywhere and nowhere at the same time. The Australian democratic theorist John Dryzek (2013) argues that he cannot keep track of the deliberative democracy literature as it has ballooned in publications over the past two decades. All of these publications are certainly not a bad thing. What I am trying to express is that the size of this epistemology's complexity continues to grow without sufficient definition, clarity and understanding.

DOI: 10.1057/9781137338662

The ultimate aim of this book is to introduce a theory of democracy that can describe the complexity of the epistemology. It will first address the literature that was responsible for this turn. These are mainly works by democratic theorists that tap into post-foundational ontologies. Consider Eckersley (2011), Muhlberger (2011), Connolly (1983), Mouffe (1999) and Laclau (2001) as good examples: they argue against the spatial and temporal limits of current understandings in democracy. They argue for more data from different times, places and languages as conditions for the establishment of necessarily tenuous foundations (e.g. post-foundations). This book will then turn to time itself arguing that democracy seems to have certain biological or evolutionary qualities. This will be contrasted with a discussion arguing against these evolutionary possibilities. In other words, that democracy is only just beginning. Chapter 4 discusses both positions. It argues that democracy is difficult to understand as the sole domain of humanity and that it was not a manifestation of Western places. Instead, democracy comes across as having a deeper and more complicated history not specifically associated with certain times and places as a majority of the literature would argue.

But before diving into a discussion of major contrasts in the literature it is crucial to establish an existing model of democracy; one that is a practical manifestation of evolutionary basic democracy (heretofore EBD). Following the example of Keane (2009), who first established monitory democracy and then devoted the remainder of the *Life and Death of Democracy* to describing it, I am placing the model up front in this introduction. This will serve to define the concept that this book seeks to explain. The model will help specify certain conditions on which EBD relies. By doing this the remainder of the book reverse engineers the model showing to the reader how the theory had come about.

Modelling to describe complexity

I, and others like Isakhan (2011 [with Stockwell]; 2012; 2012 [with Stockwell]; 2013), Keane, and Sissa, contend that the system certain Greeks came to name *demos-kratos* existed in various forms before them. These systems before the Greek had different words or no words at all describing them. But given that the word 'democracy' is of Greek origin can we actually use it in this book? If we are to speak of something that substantively predates the Greek do we need a new word? Rather than

DOI: 10.1057/9781137338662

go about inventing something new, I would prefer to state that since the word has no discernable meaning, it is technically empty and can be reappropriated to encompass phenomena before the Greek. This is possible because the Greek were defining something related to pre-existing democracy with the invention of that word. In that sense 'democracy before the Greek' is not anachronistic.

To understand the model, we need to think of democracy differently to how it is approached in the global epistemology that this book presents.[3] First, space must not be less than the entire planet. This is unusual due to the difficulty of collecting the required data to argue democracy across hundreds of languages. Works on democracy are normally associated with certain spaces within the planet and not from the entire planet itself. To understand 'the' democracy we cannot look at one or a collection of territories and then extrapolate from there. That is myopic, parochial and unfair. Drawing from specific spaces in the world is, as will come to be seen in the next chapter, insufficient to meet post-foundationalist expectations. Even the most capacious theories of democracy are parochial if we attempt to extrapolate or generalize findings from certain places onto others. For us to understand democracy we need to construct the concept with evidence from the whole planet.

A good example for this critique comes from democracy indices. The Economist Intelligence Unit Democracy Index, Polity IV, Freedom House (or Gastil) Index, and the Vanhanen Polyarchy Dataset are, like certain other indices, measuring the countries of the world for a presence or degree of democracy. What these indices are actually doing is measuring specific understandings of democracy or parameters that are thought to be necessary for democratization to occur. They are not measuring democracy itself. That is not at this time possible. It is an extrapolation of theory rooted in certain times, places and languages onto other times, places and languages that may have or have had their own manifestations of democracy. This is a long-standing issue, at times divisive, between the political scientists that put together variables for the quantification of democracy and democratic theorists who criticize the theory underlying the variables used. I argue (Gagnon, 2012) that so long as empiricists use a 'disclaimer' telling the reader what the subjectivity of their definition of democracy is, this bypasses the issue. The author and reader both gain specificity and understand that this work is measuring 'such and such' a conception of democracy rather than democracy itself.

DOI: 10.1057/9781137338662

Another good example of this is Held's (2006) models of democracy. Although a brilliant work it is by no means all-encompassing and does not succeed in defining democracy. This is not what Held sought out to do. He was concerned with describing the most widely used democratic systems. The work, however, is sometimes interpreted by readers and especially by students as being the foundational keystone for democracy itself. What Held's book does magnificently is present a certain number of describable models of democracy from certain places and times in the planet. It unfortunately leaves out massive amounts of data. That being said, I am uncertain whether a book could contain the planetary data associated with democracy. That volume would be monstrous.

The second condition of the model is that time cannot be less than the entire existence of humanity. Archaic Homo sapiens 500,000 years ago and physiologically modern humans (Homo sapiens sapiens) 200,000 years ago can be viewed as one root of democracy. And as will come to be seen in Chapter 2, time does extend prior to humanity. This second condition is again unusual for the study of democracy. The majority of works on democracy do not take this encompassing view of time. They rather stick to specific temporal periods like ancient Greece, Rome, Asia Minor (i.e. Middle East, Turkey), China, India, historical Europe, the Americas and south Pacific of the past 500 years, and parts of the globe for the past century or two. Certain temporal periods have been touted and repeated to death in the literature. This helps to explain why scholars of, for example, the French Revolution are innovating by breaking apart ostensible 'old truths'. Like the US-American political theorist John Markoff, they are forming new, more impressively complex, historical works which recognize the uncertainties of current foundational claims.

The third condition of the model is that space across time must also not be viewed as a fixed property. Human demography naturally changes according to major events like ice ages, irreversible floods, pandemics, droughts and desertifications (McGowan et al., 2012). Demography also modifies due to local anthropogenic climate changes like the deforestation that occurred on Rotorua. Empire building, which leads to mass refugee migrations,[4] and tectonic shift also affect demography. This third condition adds a dimension of complexity to any given space and time. That point is not by itself novel in the literature as thinkers do look at the effects of the aforementioned on political development. Attaching this dimension to total human time and space keeps the model to certain expectations of complexity and detail.

In order to effectively understand the model it is useful to build a visualization. If we turn our attention to point one in Figure 0.1, we see a sphere composed of squares. This is the planet earth divided into squares. I argue that we need to look into each square for data related to democracy. This helps us to evenly distribute our analytic attention to all spaces of the earth and to think of data as having to come from these places for us to build a definition of democracy. In cases like Point Nemo (the furthest point on earth away from any land), where there are no humans in residence, the square in question is not useless. It can be used to conduct research on nonhuman democratic practices in the area. As can be seen in Table 1.1, there are numerous arguments about democratic phenomena happening under the sea. The sphere is not the only way of dividing the earth into analytic squares. And there is no rule against dividing a square into a thousand squares which helps for spaces where there are numerous polities. The sphere at point one in the Figure is a conceptual example. It is how we should think of the space of democracy.

Matters become more interesting at point two in the Figure. We can raise a square and pull that square out of the sphere. When a square is fully removed it resembles a railroad spike. This is because it tapers to an end (see point number three in the Figure). Time associated with a specific space is now the fixation. The narrowest end of the taper is an approximate starting point for the Homo sapiens species. We are thought to have emerged somewhere around 500,000 years ago. The face of the spike is a specific space. The length of the spike represents the time associated with that space going back to the point of human origin. As time goes back and the taper diminishes in length, the nature of the space on the face of the spike changes. It does this to match known geological, climatic or empire shifts that affect the demography in the space. In other words, it is a method to help us understand how democracy existed for all of human time for any given space. It allows us to populate the taper with data on democracy and, to a certain extent, control for demography-related complexity.

Here is where the utility of the model becomes most apparent. Viewing the spike lengthwise, we can see that certain lines and dates are pegged along the taper. The perpendicular lines indicate that there are pieces of data. These data are mined from every possible language, and from photographs of archaeological or anthropological artefacts (prehistorical, historical and contemporary) that are thought to be associated with

DOI: 10.1057/9781137338662

democracy or a democratic way of life. In sum, the model is a data repository for anything thought to be a phenomenon of democracy for the entire planet across all human time. It is an analytic tool designed for post-foundational and positivist foundations to be reached about democracy. It also allows us to understand the complexity of *humanity's* democracy discourse.

The pieces of data that we place in the model can link together using lines. This is conditional on there being convincing enough reason to establish a correlation or causation between two or more distinct pieces of data. Nevertheless, two pieces of data from the same space separated by large amounts of time can still be linked as this fosters the genesis of hypotheses. A phylogenetic tree for democracy can be built in the same way scientists link fossils and other archaeological data. There is no particular reason that we cannot treat democracy in this way.

Although the next chapter of this book is devoted wholly to anthropogenic democracy, its second chapter describes a literature on democracy which falls outside of the human species. If we direct our attention to the end of the taper in point four in the Figure, it is easy to imagine the phylogenetic tree moving off to the right at a diagonal mirrored by 'roots' going off to the left. We can put unusual labels on those imaginary roots: microbial life, Canadian geese and cockroaches, Neanderthals, Denisovan man and chimpanzees. To these one could add certain wasp, ant and termite species, two types of mole rats, as well as slime-mould. What these imaginary roots at point four demonstrate is that there might be a deeper, nonhuman, history of basic democratic practices. These practices are arguably the best modes of social interaction for survival. In this sense, honeybees evolved the use of certain democratic practices as these worked best over millions of years of trial and error for the perpetuation of their species. Contemporary Darwinian theory (Pross, 2011) would argue that the evolution of what we interpret as a democratic practice within an insect society must be due to its effectiveness. Decision-making including quorum formation, group communication, independent thinking and changeable leadership, among other observable phenomena, are theorized to have existed well before Homo sapiens rose as a species.

If we manage to populate each square with historical and contemporary democracy it will at this stage become possible to link data across time for any given space, or at least those spaces that will have data associated with them. Antarctica, for example, would have data dating

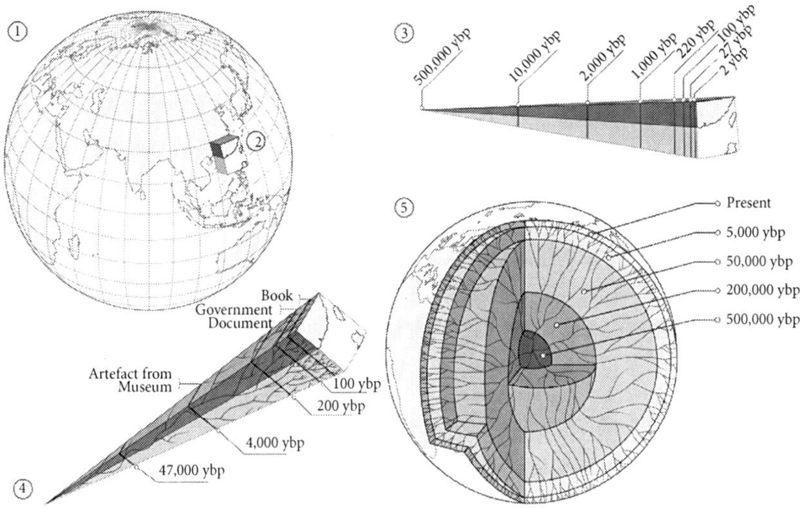

FIGURE 0.1 *A model of evolutionary basic democracy*

back a few hundred years and would, in addition to possible nonhuman democracies, have a comparatively small phylogenetic tree. As seen at point four in Figure 0.1, these efforts at linking bodies of data can create linear taxonomies of democracy. This literally builds the phylogenetic tree of planetary democracy, one temporal-spatiality at a time. That may help to explain the complex diversity of democracy today and its supposed simplicity during the dawn of Homo sapiens.

Point five in the Figure is an example of this. It shows what a global phylogenetic tree of democracy might look like. Lines are simpler in the smaller sphere associated with 500,000 years before the present (ybp) as there were not many human beings. Those that existed were in certain parts of Africa. As time advances, the taxonomy becomes more complex in the middle sphere associated with 50,000 ybp. Humans are not yet in the Americas but are in Africa, Eurasia and certain Pacific Islands. Populations are higher and modes of governance have emerged to organize large numbers of individuals living together in certain places like the Fertile Crescent. The taxonomy becomes extremely complex for the part of the sphere associated with the present time. Democracy is simple to start but becomes more complex as humanity progresses in time and space. Some would argue that actual democracy was suppressed

DOI: 10.1057/9781137338662

as this complexity grew. Democracy became the victim of imperialism, violence and elite control. Depending on the polity and the scale (i.e. federal versus municipal) citizens became subjects.

The model above succeeds in doing four things. The first is that it provides an innovative structure to place democracy data within. It permits us to start managing the complexity of the discourse. The second is that it forces the raw essence of democracy as having to be something derived from the entire existence of Homo sapiens. A definition of democracy should not come from anything less than planetary space and human time. The third, especially once the model is robustly populated, is that this database would permit reproducible scientific methods to analyse as much of what we think is democracy as possible. And the fourth is that the model will help to pin-point where in time and space the study of democracy for humans is missing. That last point may help to supercharge the discourse as temporal and spatial gap identification will be made easier for scholars of democracy.

As we need to populate the model with data from a large number of languages, times and places it will have to be a collective effort. This kind of collaboration would take time to fill the model as the discourse of democracy is enormous. The aim is to have this process occur digitally once a four-dimensional interactive model is finished and brought to life on the internet. Seeing as how a first order definition of democracy is not currently known, there should be no barrier to what can and what cannot be inserted into the model. If a convincing argument is made that this book, article, artefact or recorded phenomenon is thought to be indicative of some thinking or action associated with democracy or as having been democratic, it must be included. Although some might balk at this method, arguing that it would result in the contamination of the data by non-democratic things, I hypothesize that the weight of the evidence will converge on an objective truth. This will occur after meta-analyses are conducted on the results from numerous different reproducible studies that seek to understand the most basic shared characteristics of the data in the model. I presume that the collective outcome of these meta-analyses will be a description of a stochastic convergence (derived from the predictive side of Brownian motion) that will manifest itself within the data. This should be the positivist definition of democracy: the raw essence that we are after.

With this model in play, thinkers will be able to ask the largest and most capacious database of democracy, through multifarious research

DOI: 10.1057/9781137338662

methods, what its shared characteristics are, and to do this in ways that are reproducible. That is a core requirement to establish a positivist basic definition of democracy capable of describing how we reached this point of complexity in the epistemology. The positivist aspect of the model will make contesting arguments possible, but much more difficult given that the tenuous foundation to be reached will be one that meets scientific methods known to humans today. That kind of definition will give experts, practitioners and citizens concerned with democracy a toothy place to fight from. What is democracy or democratic will become clear in a basic sense. It will not be possible for powers to deny unless the validity of the foundation reached in the model is broadly agreed by the scientific community to have been flawed. In the end, this model is a pathway to change the politics of the world. To know, with scientific rigour, what is democracy and what is not democracy (or democratic) has wide-ranging implications.

Why does any of this matter?

The way democracy is discussed in this book is unusual. It meets the call in this book that democracy must be thought of in a substantively different way. That is probably why an anonymous expert commented that this work is a possible 'game-changer' for the field of democracy studies.

The benefits of the model above and its unusual approach to thinking about democracy indicate the importance of EBD as a theory. But this book is not intrinsically about the model. It is, rather, an introduction to how the model above came into existence. This book describes specific bodies of literature and builds up the theory of EBD. It is a critical overture. This results in a novel way of understanding the complexity of democracy. It is the description of a newer narrative foundation whose importance is exemplified by the model.

There is a small but growing literature on the subject which first began in the 1910s. Thinkers during that approximate time began to question the dogma of democracy's standard narrative. That narrative sees democracy's origins in the ancient Greek. There is, of course, *zoon politikos* from Aristotle that greatly predates the questions of democracy's origins in the 1910s. Or *bios politikos* from Hannah Arendt (2007), biopolitics from Michel Foucault (1978: 135–145) and later the politicization of life given by Giorgio Agamben (1998: 119–125) that deals with temporal

DOI: 10.1057/9781137338662

periods before the 20th century. But these are not engagements about democracy's origins. Nor are they about the human–animal from prehistory. Those works are rather an exploration of the living human–animal and her contemporaneous political existence. Life enabled or ended by politics, life defined by politics, or life transmogrified by politics. EBD is concerned with the primordial ooze of democracy. It wants to understand what democracy is in its most fundamental state. The main question is about where democracy originates. Did this happen through the existence of proto-humans before Homo sapiens started to leave fossil records? And how does this differ from literature claiming that democracy has not yet arrived?

Matters will begin with the period in time of democracy's inception. This body of literature is concerned with how democracy evolved and what its most basic, animal and human characteristics are: essentially, that which underlines all of the competing concepts and theories of democracy describable today.

Notes

1 This term is used by Schemeil to discuss non-Grecian democracy before democratic Hellas.

2 A positivist definition is one that can be established using reproducible scientific methods.

3 Please note that global epistemology means the collection of literatures concerning democracy from mainly the English literature. I have, however, conducted research in French, Russian, Spanish and Portuguese. Although these are the languages that I can work with they are insufficient in number to meet the needs of EBD. As will come to be argued, data on democracy must come from all languages for the model to work.

4 See Brather (2011) and Jennissen (2011) for evidence pertaining to the migration point in the demography argument.

DOI: 10.1057/9781137338662

1

The Subalterns and Unknowns of Democracy

Abstract: *Two bodies of literature on democracy are described in this chapter. The first concerns anthropocentric works that claim wider and different origins for democracy. The history of democracy is more complex than we currently think it is. The second body of literature described concerns nonhuman democracy. The chapter offers a table that surveys mammals, birds, fish, insects, slime-moulds and bacteria. Biologists argue that these different species have specific democratic practices. The chapter describes that physicists and mathematicians use the terms 'democracy' and 'democratic' in their works. It asks whether democracy or democratic things had a role to play in the origins of life.*

Gagnon, Jean-Paul. *Evolutionary Basic Democracy: A Critical Overture*, Basingstoke: Palgrave Macmillan, 2013.
DOI: 10.1057/9781137338662.

This chapter aims to highlight two specific bodies of literature. The first body of literature we look at gains focus in Chapter 2 and the second in Chapter 3. Chapter 4 will discuss both bodies. This results in the introduction to evolutionary basic democracy (EBD) as a theory. Of central importance is my argument that a little-known but important body of literature exists. This body covers democracies in different places during, for example, democratic Hellas, the English Revolution or the birth of the United Nations. I consider this to be a subaltern of the discourse. Further below I discuss a key point regarding hybridity and how this affects foundational claims. But to get to these two literatures we must first explain where they originate. Paine and Muhlberger (1993: 25, 26) help to set the tone:

> Two factors have allowed historians, political theorists, and others to represent democratic theory or practice as uniquely western phenomena: ignorance, and the concentration of historical research on the largest and best recorded institutions. That many historians know little about history outside of Europe and North America needs no demonstration ... [Historians looking to places and times outside of the West] have seen only a mass of churlish and intractable peasants, too dumb to understand voting or the principle of human equality, now or ever.

There is a dominant body of literature that places the origins of democracy undoubtedly within ancient Hellas. It is to this body that Paine and Muhlberger (1993: 25, 26) address their critique. This literature argues that democracy after Greece was carried into the present by the items on the following list:

- the Roman Republic (Ikeskamp and Heitmann-Gordon, 2010: 4, 20; Millar, 1998: 4);
- the ecclesiastical practices of certain religions like Christianity and Islam (Papanikolaou, 2003: 95; Khatab and Bouma, 2007);
- the decision-making practices of Italian City-States (Jones, 1997);
- Arabic scholars (al-Jabri, 2008; Abdalla and Rane, 2011);
- Germanic and Swiss customs like the *Märzfeld* or *Landsgemeinde* (Head, 1995; Mellor, 2010: 15);
- Nordic *things* – pronounced 'tings' (Boulhosa, 2011);
- European *wieches, sejms* and *folkmoots* along with their cognates (Barnwell and Mostert, 2003);
- guilds of all sorts (Arjomand, 2004: 324);
- the Isle of Man's *Tynwald* which is thought to be the world's oldest parliament (Edge and Pearce, 2006);

DOI: 10.1057/9781137338662

- Ireland's *Tuáth* (Canny, 2010);
- the *elisate* of the Basque nation (Ugarte, 2009);
- the rise of aristocracies from the Balkans and Eastern Europe to Ireland and Iceland that devolved power from autocrats and monarchs (Congleton, 2011);
- the seemingly sacred Magna Charta (Wood, 1969: 537);
- the innovations during the English, French and American revolutions (Gill, 2008);
- New England town hall meetings (Robinson, 2011);
- the 20th century's successive triumphs of democracy over fascism, totalitarianism, communism and other non-democratic rule (Huntington, 1991);
- and the 21st century's e-democracy which some argue brought the demoi more transparency and accountability among other things (Insua and French, 2010).

Even though the list above is over-simplistic we should consider that this story is true insofar as the aforementioned items are actually about specific types of western Eurocentric democracy. And these democracies differ from one another in a number of ways. For example, there was not a gradual rise of aristocrats across the world. Not even in Europe. Nothing led to the dissolution of some terrible autocratic age because that homogeneous time did not exist. As far as we can tell, depending on the society observed, there were large numbers of aristocratic strenghtenings *and* weakenings depending on who was alive when, what transpired and how. In short, polities differ from each other in history but suffer the homogenizing effects that certain historical narratives have.

Black (2009: 1–2) is a good example of this homogenizing narrative. He argues that:

> Sociology has long been inter-cultural. World history is at last coming into its own. But in the history of ideas, globalization still has some way to go. While histories of Western political thought, usually starting with the ancient Greeks, abound, there are few histories of political thought in other civilizations. And there is none of the ancient world taken as a whole. This is astounding, when one considers that the period covered in this book was the most eventful in the whole history of political thought: it was then that political philosophy was invented (independently) in China and Greece; political science was invented in Greece; statecraft in China and India. Democracy and liberty (as every schoolboy or -girl perhaps knows) began in ancient Greece. Israel led directly to Judaism, indirectly to Christianity and Islam.

DOI: 10.1057/9781137338662

Black (2009) recognized that the globalization of ancient political history is only just beginning. But as the reader will see many of the claims Black makes above are patently false. This is especially evident regarding his argument that Greece invented political science, liberty and democracy. His book paints a picture of specific ancient places in ways that appear dramatically myopic. Black argues that Egypt, Mesopotamia, India and China were devoid of democracy. In light of recent evidence, his arguments are too broad and fall to pieces.

The same can be argued about the rise and fall of non-elites. Head (1995), Boulhosa (2011) and Barnwell and Mostert (2003) tell that the strength of non-elites grew or fell depending on how politics evolved. A non-elite assembly on the Hungarian steppes might be forced to give power to a regional autocrat. But a different assembly may not face these troubles because a mountain range protects it from more powerful militaries.

The list above is not exhaustive as the definition of specific bodies in the literature is subjective. The list itself might actually be too broad. The dominant literature is seen as a myopic, parochial and sometimes racist. Some say that it is an orientalist narrative. This is why a different scholar like Paine (with Muhlberger, 1993) would probably remove Nordic *things* and northern European non-elite assemblies like *folkmoots* or *wieches* from the list. He would note that they are not on average included in the bulk of democracy's history. Keane (2012a) would probably remove Arabic scholars as they were and still are ignored in the dominant historical record of democracy. Leaving *things* and Arabic scholars on that list might give unfair virtue to a narrative that has otherwise colonized the discourse of democracy.

A good explanation about why some view this narrative so unhappily comes from Paine. The French, German and English literatures during the 19th and 20th centuries were conservative. They were blatantly opposed to the idea of democracies that differed from ancient Athens or its north Atlantic revolutionary origins. Anything else in that western European time-space could not be democratic because Greece invented it and Europe carried the torch forward. The blinders came onto the discourse early and we have only just begun removing them. Indeed, Thomas (1990: 310) supports this point in his discussion of the poet William Wordsworth:

> [For Wordsworth] to speak thus in praise of democracy and democratic principles, even so late as 1820, was a bold move. The word democracy, even

DOI: 10.1057/9781137338662

> then, still had very negative connotations, for most people, of violence and radicalism and mob rule. But Wordsworth was not afraid to use the word, for he was one of the most profound and entire believers in democracy who ever lived and wrote. In 1794, when he was barely 24, he announced boldly, even defiantly, 'I am of that odious class of men called democrats, and of that class I shall for ever continue'.

Democracy in this example is held in contempt due to the contemporaneous belief that it was dangerous or distasteful. Thomas' example helps to illustrate how humans can hold democracy sacred or profane depending on how they understand the concept.

Others like Elstub (2010), Levy (2010), Curato (2012) and Marktanner and Nasr (2009) might add to the list. They would cite the recent growth in popularity of deliberative and de-militarized democracies. Elstub, Levy and Curato argue that deliberative democracy is a core practice for any democracy to work. Levy, for example, details how deliberation fosters better public law. For Marktanner and Nasr, militaries are possibly anathema to democracy. This is a position that I agree with as I would prefer to see the enlisted and reservists placed in border security, police, search and rescue, and to continue building the international corps of peacekeepers.

In short, the dominant literature on democracy's evolution is not strictly defined. Nor do the literatures I associate with each item on the list necessarily get along. Curato (2011) for example would not argue that democracy originates solely from the 'West'. But we can make a general statement that the bulk of the literature argues that one or more of the items I list above are essential for democracy to exist.

An easy-to-spot problem is that the narrative in this major body of literature is a western Eurocentric one. Even eastern European or Russian scholars are not typically given any credit toward innovations in democracy. In the case of Arabic scholars, certain historic individuals who spoke or who were Arabic are considered to be those handy scholars who retained Greek writings. Greek works via Arabic were translated into Latin and subsequently a plurality of European languages. This is the main explanation for how democracy disappeared from the world only to be rediscovered. It is difficult to think that democracy exchanged hands in that exact manner (from Arabic to Latin to French for example), although the historical record maintains that it happened that way (Isakhan, 2012: 15). In this narrative, historical Arabic democratic theory has no place. Arabs were only translators – nothing more. That

DOI: 10.1057/9781137338662

point helps us to understand why the existing narrative of democracy is considered orientalist. Arabs in history thought about democracy. The English discourse is only beginning to access this important ontology.

To round this portrayal off we should recognize that this literature, despite its massive size, is still a patchy portrayal of just a western European typology of democracy. It seems unreasonable, if not irrational, to think that the rest of the world and the humans living therein were not participants in democracy's evolution. To borrow the words of Yves Schemeil there is a history of democracy *before* democracy. Humans were already present on every continent save for Antarctica during the time of democratic Hellas. Barring the forthcoming evidence that shows Hellas not to have invented democracy, probability would see types of democracy emerging in various forms wherever humans are found. Black (2009) argues that these early human societies are egalitarian and not democratic. But should we look at Black's conception of democracy, it is inescapably subjective and falls prey to the logic of his own critique. Since we do not know what democracy is how can we pass judgment on what others are not?

The discourse presented above is unfortunately still the dominant one in the literature. It will also not gain any further focus in this book. Rather, we will look at a specific tranche in that body. This is the second body of literature described in this chapter. It is associated with times and places that argue between one another over what 'true', 'real', 'actual', 'existing' or 'substantive' democracy is and where first democracy originated.

The third and final body of literature we look at champions the criticisms and conditions that I made in the paragraphs above. The language of this body of literature is unusual. It is closer to the one used in the Introduction. It asks whether democracy existed well before 'democracy' was coined by an undetermined Greek, African or Mesopotamian. It asks about the evolution of that form of politics and looks for its origins in Kropotkin's cooperation over competition argument. Pyotr Alexeyevich Kropotkin had, after his work in Siberia during the later 1800s, published *Mutual Aid: A Factor of Evolution* in 1902. In this work Kropotkin argues that it was cooperation, rather than competition, which drove the survival of species. From microbes in pond scum, to animal societies in brutal winters, to human societies in challenging conditions, cooperation is observable in ways that contradict the obvious advantages gained through competition. I consider this third body to be an unknown dimension in the discourse of democracy.

DOI: 10.1057/9781137338662

This unknown literature involves the works of biologists, archaeologists, anthropologists, neuroscientists, historians and democratic theorists. It looks to indigenous peoples, to Africa, to Asia, to the Pacific, to the Americas and to nonhumans during, before and after ancient Hellas, the English Revolution and the birth of the United Nations. The story of democracy in this body of literature breaks down previous barriers. It argues that the phenomena described in the democratic states of ancient Hellas were also known in similar forms to city-states in India. They were known to villages in Papua New Guinea or the Ituri Forest and in Iroquoian or Wendat cultures. Some argue that the Greek ideal of collective decision-making through independent thinking appears to be known to *Apis mellifera*, or the European honeybee (Seeley, 2011, 2013). It is a wide open and in many ways a wonderful new world of democracy.

But before progressing, we must note that the preferential emphasis given to the small emergent literature does not disparage the existing dominant Eurocentric ontology. It is simply a recontextualization. Hellenistic democratic typology becomes not the first origin of democracy but rather a mutation of something that predated it: a mutation that brought, and still brings, a bounty to contemporary democratic theory and practice. The same can be said about the morphologies of representative democracy that came impressively out of the English, French and American revolutions.

We first look to what Isakhan and Stockwell (2011) coin as the 'standard history of democracy'. This is not a mundane repetition of evidence paraded in sequence and designed to match the list in the first paragraph of this chapter. Rather, it is a body of evidence critically discussing the nuanced evolution of democracy in that narrative. That offers a different spin on what is at times a stale discussion. Nevertheless, for those readers who are not intimately familiar with democracy's more common historical narrative, the following works should bring us sufficiently up to speed in order to appreciate the discussion launched in the next paragraph: Arblaster (2002), Estlund (2002), Crick (2002), Dunn (2005), Weale (2007), Tilly (2007) and Saward (2003, 2006).

Origins in antiquity, revolutions, suffrage and beyond

There is something of an unwritten custom in the literature which sees scholars state, rather dogmatically, that the Greek were the creators of

DOI: 10.1057/9781137338662

democracy and the first political culture. Ehrenberg (1950) and Fleck and Hanssen (2006) are good examples of this. But there are others who examine Grecian origins. They describe the delicate evidence and build certain foundational claims rather than stating in one way or the other that Athens *is* the cradle of democracy (Mitchell-Boyask, 2009: 374; Roe, 2002: 123). These, and works that argue for other Eurocentric democratic origins, are the ones we look at.

As seen in the list I provided at the beginning of this chapter, this literature on democracy has numerous starting points. It is not a linear continuation. And in many ways it is a group of moral works which typically reject previous forms of democracy. The definition of the citizenry and the regulated behaviour of agents in the Pnyx for Athens were possibly sufficient for certain individuals to scorn the looser, more inclusive, decision-making style of Chaonia. The ability for women to vote and run for office, and the extension of citizenship to un-propertied men as well as to teenagers, is as some would argue the mark of actual democracy. That last point disqualifies most historical democracies, including some Swiss cantons up until the late 20th century, from being democratic. And for others still, the vote, the right to run for office and the foundational institutions of representative systems are totally insufficient for democracy.

There are scholars who argue that on top of a widening franchise there must be one or more from the list below for democracy to exist or function:

- more options for inclusive participation (Young, 2002; Pateman, 2012);
- more assemblies with higher deliberative and discursive quality (Dryzek and Niemeyer, 2008);
- less corruption (Della Porta and Mény, 1997), more transparency (Haug, 2001) and greater accountability (Bukhari and Haq, 2010) which can now together be expressed as 'more monitorism' (Keane, 2009);
- more knowledgeable, critical, political interest from citizens (Rapeli, 2012, 2013);
- greater numbers of referenda and electronic voting (Lake and Sosin, 1998; Yao and Murphy, 2007);
- better regulation of corporations by the demos or that benefit the demos (Barley, 2007);

DOI: 10.1057/9781137338662

- more impressive representation (Alonso et al., 2011);
- reformed electoral campaigns (Birch, 2011);
- less 'trash' media and better policed media (Bertrand, 2003; Cohen, 2005);
- basic training on voting for citizens and standardized testing for politicians (Gagnon, 2012b);
- and greater ease of access to politics for one or more citizens enabling them to advance with whatever issue they might have (Hay, 2007).

For many today one or more items from the list above qualifies as a must for a democracy to be democratic. Or, theoretically, for democracy to exist. If we take the aforementioned requirements and look at any commonly regarded democratic polity, I contend that all would be failures. The City of Toronto, the state of Queensland, the USA, the EU, and the General Assembly of the United Nations would each struggle to meet everything on the list above. The best of the group would amount to trying in certain places to create the sparks needed to start the democratic fire. In that light, democracy does not exist today. It has never existed – but it is on the horizon. As will come to be seen, this body of literature is an importantly disjointed story of many democracy claimants across numerous times and spaces.

Dandamayev (1995) and Isakhan (2012) establish a pre-Hellenistic starting point for democracy. They focus on Ancient Iraq or Mesopotamia because the earliest evidence on democracy can be tied to those places.

> When the Mesopotamian state first emerged in the early periods, royal power did not play an important role and only many centuries later did it become despotic. Originally kings were merely the first among equals and were obliged by laws or by long social traditions to respect the rights of the population. In addition, royal power was restricted by popular assemblies which sometimes had a real and even decisive influence and which made citizens proud of their civil rights (Dandamayev in Isakhan, 2012: 40).

Isakhan offers evidence of god myths, the epics of Enmarkar, Lugalbanda, and Gilgamesh. These are important as they revolve around human or semi-human protagonists, and arguments about the independent city-states of Sumerian civilization among much else. It is a weighty argument that states a broad culture of democracy existed some 2,400 years before democratic Hellas. One god myth is particularly worth retelling. Isakhan (2012: viv) sheds light on the 'democratic practices of the Ordained Assembly of the Great Gods that the myth of Enuma Elish reveals'.

> The council was made up of 50 gods and goddesses in total and together they constituted the Ordained Assembly of the Great Gods. This assembly was called together when the gods needed to make the decisions regarding any number of issues and constituted the highest authority in the universe.

A second example of pre-Hellenistic democratic possibilities lies with Schemeil's (2000) work. It pulls apart ways of understanding democracy in ancient times. Schemeil argues that Pharaonic Egypt and Mesopotamian cultures like Sumer and Assyria were places of 'public debate and detailed voting procedures; countless assemblies convened at the thresholds of public buildings or city gates'. They were places where disputed trials were submitted to higher courts among other arguably democratic practices. This extends to the Cycladic, Minoan and Mycenaean civilizations which are predecessors to the pan-Greek culture. That evidence suggests two main arguments. The first is that Hellas may have grown culturally due to complex societal evolutions coming out of previous civilizations. The second is that the Greek typology of democracy may have been the result of innovations on pre-existing democracy systems from north-east Africa, the Fertile Crescent and south-east Europe.

Hybrid theory in Latour (1994), Urry (2006) and Haraway (2006) play are role in Schemeil's arguments. Hybridity and complexity relate to comments made in the Introduction about how classicists are re-engaging Athenian and Greek democratic foundations. Although north-east Africa, south-east Europe, the Fertile Crescent and the Mediterranean basin are places, they cannot be static entities. They were not something at one point in time independent of past times. They were not places independent of previous human movement, of the diffusion of ideas and practices shared through even the most rudimentary forms of communication. I argue that the Hellenistic typology of democracy, which had multifarious democratic praxes, must have been dependent on broader and more complicated histories. It is unlikely that the practice of assembling individual human beings for the purpose of reaching collective decisions was invented by Athens or other Greek states. It does not make sense.

Hybridity forces a discussion on first democracy whether that be Greek, French, global, pre-historical or otherwise. Democracy even 500,000 years ago would not have been a eureka moment to one woman in an animal skin shelter. Homo sapiens' democracy came from somewhere else. It came from primates. Continuing in that vein, the democratic traits in insect societies had origins. And those origins had origins. Democracy might be a condition of life itself which is a notion not removed from empirical reality. Humans have developed the capacity to create artificial life and are describing in increasingly impressive ways which inanimate conditions are needed for animate matter to spontaneously 'live'. Do amino acids work cooperatively to create basic microbial life? Is the physical inanimate universe a place of cooperation rather than competition? Or both as it appears to be with sperm? The duality between cooperation and competition is too simplistic. Democracy could need both or possibly be a result of both – or a third, fourth of fifth set of unknown variables.

These are astronomical questions turned to later in the book. At this stage we need to refocus hybridity for the second body of literature. The central point to take away from this part of the discussion is that any foundational claim for first democracy cannot be viewed in a vacuum. Even the most radical arguments of democracy are muddled, complex and linked to other things. They all take from somewhere, move from somewhere, are innovated from somewhere, contrast against something and through that reinforce the likelihood of there being a raw essence of democracy. Follett (1965 [c1920]) and Wright (1949) argue the point of democracy's ever changing meaning. But they do not specify that change in meaning can happen independently from the historical record as Latour (1994) does. Democracy comes from somewhere but it is not as the historical record currently presents it.

Raflaub, Ober and Wallace (2007) provide a Grecian starting point. The contributors to their volume question possible points of origin for democracy. They offer the view that the Greek may have been innovating within an already established culture of resistance to power. There may have been previous forms of collective decision-making and conceptions of citizenship among much else. The book does not however advance in that direction but stays within Hellas. To offer an example of what Raflaub, Ober and Wallace probably meant, Stockwell (2011a) spoke of Phoenician democracy. This was a type of mobile, trading and ship-based system of collective governance. It may have started one thousand years or more before Athens began its experiments in government. Raflaub, Ober and Wallace do not go to those lengths. This might be the case because the archaic historical record of early Greek democracies offers even less evidence than what is available to scholars of less dated periods in ancient Hellas.

DOI: 10.1057/9781137338662

Greek democracy is in itself contested. The first Greek democracy is not definitively known. We only know the earliest record which comes from Herodotus' *Histories* (1996 [460 BCE]). Grecian democracy did not have full suffrage. Athens and Sparta were based on types of slavery and were militaristic places. Scholars today argue that this disqualifies Athens and Sparta from having been democratic. Theirs were different forms of government: oligarchies, patriarchies or military regimes.

The descriptive issues in ancient Hellas are a starting point for a tradition of arguing that democracy has its origins in later times. Gillin (1919) is central to understanding this contestation of origins. He argues, well before the late 1940s where the practice of viewing democracy globally re-emerged in the English discourse, that democracy's beginnings came from early human societies. During that time villages, or collections of villages, would have numbered not more than a few hundreds or thousands of individuals. For Gillin this is the birth of ways that societies carried themselves culturally. It is where later civilizations from 10,000 or 20,000 years ago had the ideas to hold assemblies at city gates, or for leaders to consult some sort of council. This is true even in ostensibly oppressive regimes. It is the perspective that there was not a lightning bolt which struck a prehistorical genius that then led to a fundamental shift in ways of doing government or governance.

The act of individuals assembling and discussing matters that are pressing to their collective welfare was not an invention. Gillin may have thought that this was a natural inclination for humans. I think that is clear in his discussion of how democracy was oppressed with nation-state or empire building. This point is also clear in his discussion of how democracy mutated in places that resisted empire and how it later came into vogue once more: when societies continued questioning class divisions, inequalities and sovereign oppression.

Gillin writes that democracy became increasingly suppressed in places that succumbed to autocracy. That it grew and found new origins as it mutated in places like Sumerian city-states or hunter-gatherer cultures in African forests. Democracy flourished and stuttered and stopped depending on which case across a specific time and space, or series of times and spaces, we look to. This helps to explain why debates in the dominant literature about origins are increasingly common. Scholars decipher the Greek typology, or the Italian, French, American and global typologies to argue that these places in time achieved the beginnings of true democracy. But these, as argued above, are again the true beginnings

DOI: 10.1057/9781137338662

of different types of democracy linked to complexity across animate and inanimate matter. At the same time they still share common characteristics which it appears Gillin had been pointing to nearly a century ago.

To round this description of literature off, Sader (2010) writes that for many Latin Americans in the late 1950s and early 1960s, the USA had been seen as the *cuna de la democracia* or the cradle of democracy. Magalhães (2000: 141) supports this point. Frank (1999: 53) writes the 'cradle of democracy in the United Kingdom ...' which was also argued by Labutina (1994). Reichardt (1994) states that Germany's uptake of democracy was directly caused by the French Revolution and the interpretations of democracy it fostered or forced to have reconsidered. Dirmoser (2005) argues that democracies in Latin America are effectively substanceless: they are democracies without democracy. Examples like these are numerous across a number of languages, although most works do take a historical approach to democracy and not one that wholly rejects previous forms. As will come to be seen in Chapter 3, that type of a priori rejection is found in a specific tranche of the literature.

Origins on the edge of time, space and species

Above I describe at least two bodies of literature on the history of democracy. The first is the dominant narrative. It typically presents a story starting from ancient Hellas. The narrative tracks western Eurocentric democracy falsely as democracy itself and uses this history as a foundation for contemporary research on democracy – especially in empirical works. The second and smaller body of literature argues for completely separate origins of democracy. It started here and stopped there; it began with such and ended so.

For the foundational claims that originate democracy in antiquity, the linear narrative is present as thinkers argue democracy to have continued after its birth. But the narrative we look at, especially in Chapter 3, is different from those taking Athens as a starting point. Parpola (2000: 29–30) helps to explain:

> [I]n comparison with Greek and Hellenistic cultures, Mesopotamian culture at first sight, undeniably, seems alien and strange. The better one has learned to understand it, however, the more it has come to resemble our own culture. Its strange and exotic features conceal within themselves an invisible world of ideas more familiar to us, which resurfaces in new garments

DOI: 10.1057/9781137338662

> but largely identical in content in classical antiquity. In Mesopotamia, the visible and invisible worlds were connected with each other through a complex system of symbols, images, metaphors, allegories and mental associations. Unravelling this symbolic code opens the way to the very core of Mesopotamian culture, the world of ideas hidden [in] its conventional and alien surface.

From this example we can see that ancient Mesopotamia, at least as we understand it today, is not so different in social makeup to many contemporary societies. This automatically broadens the linear narrative beyond the standard one. Mesopotamia as origin for democracy and not initially Athens? Perhaps democracy in the 20th century BCE tracked further east. Maybe it came even earlier than that from forests in Africa or across trading routes from the Indian subcontinent. Different historical foundations for democracy change the spatial boundaries of its progressive narrative into the present.

But for those who work with contemporary moral philosophy, all previous democracies were attempts at being democratic. The real deal has not yet arrived, or, if it has arrived, this has happened only recently. Others say that only parts of democracy have arrived. There are many continuing struggles to achieve full or true democracy. See Huntington (1991), Lijphart (2001) and Fukuyama (2010, 2012) for examples that discuss democracy in this ontology. The second body offers a much broader account of origination. It focuses on a specific period rather than arguing one period to have been merely the result of a predecessor and then linking that to a successor.

The third body of literature is an entirely different, dislocated and unusual body of literature on democracy. It argues about things that are thought to be democratic. It shines a light in unusual places. These are works that appear outside of democratic theory and political or social philosophy. They have little to no presence in empirical political science. This literature comes from biology, microbiology, medicine and the 'hard' sciences like physics and mathematics. As Tribe (1989: 2) argues, the 'metaphors and intuitions that guide physicists can enrich our comprehension of social and legal issues'. We investigate the sciences then to see what we can learn from them and to see whether this has value for the study of democracy.

Starting with physics and maths which are fields in the business of describing the entire universe, we run into a number of surprising terms:

- 'Dimensionally democratic calculus' (Pezzaglia, 1999);
- 'Wrapping democracy' (Rador, 2005);
- 'Democratic algorithm' (Koide and Fusaoka, 2002);
- 'Democratic superstring field theory' (Kroyter, 2011);
- 'Democratic-type model' (Miura et al., 2000);
- 'Democratic mass matrix' (Haba et al., 2000);
- 'Democratic module PV system' (Itoh et al., 2001);
- 'Flavor democracy'; (Sultansoy, 2006);
- 'Quantum democracy' (Segre, 2010);
- and 'Democratic neutrinos' (Karl and Simpson, 2002).

Depending on how a person defines democracy, the use of 'democracy' and 'democratic' in these fields has nothing to do with the way these terms are understood in the study of politics. As physicist Gerard Milburn stated, physicists have a habit of borrowing words from other fields to use them in completely different ways. As we will come to see in the next chapter, this is corroborated by a number of interviews I have with physicists that use this language in their works. Until, that is, we reach the point of asking whether atoms, micro-particles and celestial bodies might actually be observed as operating in 'democratic' ways. That reaches into the philosophy of physics where Meierhenrich (2008) plays a role.

Going from inanimate matter to specific types of living things, or animate matter, the literature has a small bounty to offer. To start, there is the growing experimental literature that relates to synaptic or dendritic democracy (Rumsey and Abbott, 2006; Gidon and Segev, 2009; Sterratt and Ooyen, 2004). Neuroscientists argue that independent synapses work collectively. In other words, there is an argument to make about democracy in the brain. There is also evidence suggesting that individual genes in plants form a consensus on how to collectively behave in response to a stressor like cold (Benedict et al., 2006). The article explains that genes have a voting mechanism which dictates how a plant will respond to the stressor in question.

This kind of research has already begun impacting arguments in political philosophy. We can see this with Coles' (2011: 273) argument that 'mirror neurons [disclose] ways in which iterated practices and dispositional structures are crucial for democratic freedom'. We are trying to make political arguments for humans from what synapses do in animal (human and nonhuman) neural networks. That, importantly, is done similarly with the democracies observed in social insect societies.

DOI: 10.1057/9781137338662

The American biologist Thomas Seeley (2011, 2013), for example, argues that human democracy can benefit from studying nonhuman democracy. This will be turned to with greater detail in the next chapter.

The use of 'democracy' in biology appeared as early as 1979. Kacser and Burns (1979: 1149) used it in the following way which helps to set the tone for our coming discussion:

> A Democratic Society is difficult to define. Neither are all [persons] equal nor are all governed by a single [person]. The Society works by the interaction of many different kinds of [people], groups, interests and powers. Molecular Society is not that different. There are a large number of molecular species which interact with one another, some catalysing, some being catalysed, some combining, some splitting, some inhibiting, some activating, and some doing several of these at the same time. The system works as it does because of the interactions of the molecules ...

Welch and Keleti (1987) were also writing similarly almost a decade later. In their criticism of Kacser and Burns, they used words like 'enzymo-democracy', 'molecular society' and 'supramolecular socialism'. But it was Conradt and Roper (2007) who strengthened the drive in the natural sciences to look for democracies in animate matter. 'Consider a group of primates', they argued

> deciding where to travel after a rest period, a flock of birds deciding when to leave a foraging patch or a swarm of bees choosing a new nest site; unless all members decide on the same action, some will be left behind and will forfeit, at least temporarily, the advantages of group living. Thus, in order to maintain group cohesion, social animals – like humans – have to make consensus decisions, chiefly about the timing and nature of activities and about future travel destinations. Moreover, as in humans, consensus decisions in animals often lead to conflict of interest between group members, owing to the fact that individual members often differ with respect to their optimal activity budgets. (Conradt and Roper, 2007: 2317)

These kinds of work are central to the growing discussions in political ecology about 'representing nature'. This 'greening' of democracy (Keane 2013, 2013a; Gagnon 2012a) is one of the fastest growing areas in contemporary democratic theory. As Latour (1994), Eckersley (2011), and Dobson (2010) among others have argued, when scientists 'listen' to baboons, or when ecologists 'speak' for the trees, they are not only making human representations of nonhumans but are also engaging in a dialogue that takes place between humans and nonhumans. It links

DOI: 10.1057/9781137338662

back to hybridity and arguments stating the unlikelihood of separating democracy from nature.

Given that the literature on animate nonhuman democracy is larger than that associated with inanimate matter, I put Table 1.1 together to showcase a broad sample of this literature. Directing our attention to Table 1.1, directly below, a survey of animate nonhuman democratic life is presented.

Notice that I purposely use broad labels for the animate creatures featured in Table 1.1. I do this to designate that the field of better understanding the *culture* of animals has only recently begun. It is likely that a majority of animate creatures have cultures. And that culture exists between species. But pushing arguments beyond this foundation is unsustainable. There is not enough evidence to go into that direction. We will have to see how the literature plays out over the coming decades.

One interesting point comes from Reuvan and Eldar (2011: 759–760). They make mention of bacteria being able to sense quorums and to commit altruistic suicide. An individual bacterium seems able to decide to press its own self-destruct button for the greater good. Ben-Jacob (2008) adds to this by demonstrating that bacteria form complex colonies through chemotactic signalling and the exchange of genetic information. This can happen between species of bacteria (Federle and Bassler, 2003). Quorum detection, communication, social learning and altruistic suicide occur in microbes numbering millions of 'individuals'. If we consider this to be a type of democratic society it points to the effectiveness of democracy. This may be one theory backing why bacteria learn quickly about antibiotics and change in response to their killer. Certain democratic behaviours allow bacteria to quickly change. For example, *Streptococcus mutans* is a bacterium commonly found in human oral cavities. It is associated with tooth decay. It can in this light be argued that a bacterial democratic society is present in the human mouth, and that it is responsible for keeping the profession of dentistry in good business.

These animals each have the ability to make decisions, or accept decisions, collectively. Some are able to communicate better than others. Honeybees and certain bacteria can form quorums leading to quicker decision-making. Others, like a type of yellowtail fish, form social stratifications that change as the fish age. We must take note that the discussion of nonhuman democracy is contentious. The major counter-argument is that we cannot make sophisticated objective statements about nonhuman culture. Any judgment on nonhuman culture must be subjective. It

DOI: 10.1057/9781137338662

TABLE 1.1 *Examples of nonhuman species that have observable democratic behaviour*

Land (over and under)	Mostly in the air	Mostly in the water	Microscopic
Red deer (Conradt and Roper, 2007)	Pigeons (Nagy et al., 2010)	Guppies (Reader et al., 2003)	Quorum-sensing bacteria (Adler and Tso, 1974)
African buffalo (Prins, 1996)	Canadian geese (Raveling, 1969)	Nine-spined stickleback (Kendal et al., 2008)	African trypanosome (Oberholzer et al., 2010)
Bonobos (Rosati and Hare, 2012)	Hawks (Maransky and Bildstein, 2001)	Three-spined stickleback (Frommen and Bakker, 2004)	Streptococcus mutans (Reuven and Eldar, 2011)
Ants (Mallon et al., 2001)	Swans (Black, 1988)	Yellowtail (Sakakura and Tsukamoto, 1999)	Dictyostelium discoideum (Brown and Buckling, 2008)
Macaques (Reinhardt et al., 1987)	Wire-tailed manakins (Ryder et al., 2008)	Salmonids (Brännäs et al., 2001)	Yeast (Smukalla et al., 2008)
Baboons (King and Sueur, 2011)	Honeybees (Seeley, 2011)	Turtles (Davis and Burghardt, 2011)	Cyanobacteria (Villareal, 2009)
Chimpanzees (King and Sueur, 2011)	Wasps (Karsai and Wenzel, 2000)	Porpoise (Sakai et al., 2011)	Multicellular metazoan (Villareal, 2009)
Cockroaches (Lihoreau et al., 2012)	Bats (Shwartz, 2010)	Tropical damselfish (Manassa and McCormick, 2012)	Paenibacillus (Ben-Jacob, 2008)
Naked mole rat (Bennett and Faulkes, 2000)	Crows (Holzhaider et al., 2011)	Perch (Helfman, 1984)	Genetic parasites (Villareal, 2009)
Termites (Korb, 2008)	Sparrows (Tóth et al., 2009)	Dolphins (Rendell and Whitehead, 2001)	Eukaryotes (Randerson, 2003)
Wolves (Mech and Boitani, 2003)	Red-winged fairy wren (Russell and Rowley, 2000)	Whales (Würsig, 1988)	Mycoplasma mycoides (Adami et al., 2000)

reflects observer bias if the observer is looking for, or is naturally inclined to, democracy. As we do not know what democracy is we cannot state its presence in nonhumans. Because we think of contemporary democracies as more sophisticated than nonhuman democracies we view the latter

DOI: 10.1057/9781137338662

with prefixed adjectives. Primitive democracy, proto- quasi- nonhuman-democracy, and basic- simple- raw-democracy are examples.

Although the last point may be viewed by certain biologists as the result of anthropocentric egotism, it at least gives recognition that non-humans can work in ways that humans can consider democratic. That is of central importance to the theory of evolutionary basic democracy to which we will return later.

In total, this body of literature challenges the temporality of democracy – driving it back millions, if not billions of years. Democratic behaviours happen in microscopic societies found in human blood or in the total dark, underground, as mole rats would have it. This changes the spatial dimensions of democracy. Finally, this literature pushes the boundaries of democracy well beyond Homo sapiens and into many other species or types of life.

The main question is whether these animal societies can be considered democratic at all. Can democracy be all of these things? It is difficult, if entirely improbable, to answer this question without having a positivist definition of democracy. That being said, I think it is uncontroversial enough to state that animals may certainly have types of democratic behaviour and that these are understandably evolutionary traits. One critical point that needs attention is whether these democratic things are 'democratic' at all: are they not simply altruistic behaviours? In response to this I argue that altruism is an ethos of democracy. Things that are democratic are considered altruistic. To get out of that circularity then, we can argue that democratic behaviours are evolutionary manifestations in support of communal altruistic behaviour. It is to this idea of biological evolution that we now turn to in the next chapter – starting with inanimate matter.

DOI: 10.1057/9781137338662

2
Arguments for Evolutionary Democracy

Abstract: *I investigate the sciences for their use of the terms 'democracy' and 'democratic'. Findings suggest that particles do not behave in democratic ways as they are driven by strict forces. The key is to investigate whether these forces allow for 'democratic' things to manifest when unicellular life emerges from the 'prebiotic soup'. A small selection of eusocial and social nonhumans like gametes, crows and bonobos are described. We see that nonhumans do not practice complex democracy. Rather, nonhumans have perfected specific behaviours that we as humans explain as 'democratic' behaviours. A discussion follows arguing that evidence supports the idea of an underlying basic democracy. We should look to nonhuman democratic specialization to see what we can borrow from them to use in our moral systems.*

Gagnon, Jean-Paul. *Evolutionary Basic Democracy: A Critical Overture*, Basingstoke: Palgrave Macmillan, 2013.
DOI: 10.1057/9781137338662.

 DOI: 10.1057/9781137338662

This chapter approaches the argument of democracy's evolution in the way scientists approach the formation of the earth and the human. We first look at old things: particles, prebiotics, amino acids and cellular life forms like sperm. Our main question is whether any of these things in theory or observation behave in 'democratic' ways. If, for example, prebiotics and amino acids are thought to cooperate to form life, all animate matter may then owe its existence to a democratic practice. As far as I can determine the literature on the subject of 'democracy within the atom' or its cognates does not exist. That makes it necessary for the first part of this chapter to use interviews with leading minds in the field. It is exploratory work. This chapter then introduces more complex nonhuman democratic practices like those found in slime-moulds, bonobos and crows. There is a substantive literature on the behaviour of these animals but little debate about what these democratic animal cultures mean for democracy.

The ontology of evolutionary basic democracy (EBD) becomes more complex at this juncture. As with our discussion of hybridity earlier in the work, Latour (1994: 795) is also central here.

> I [...] want to show that the tyranny of the dichotomy between humans and nonhumans is not inevitable because it is possible to give at least one other myth in which it plays no role. If I succeed in giving some space for the imagination, this would mean that we are not forever stuck with the boring alternation of humans to nonhumans and back. It would be possible to imagine a space, that will later be studied empirically, in which we could observe the swapping of properties without always having to start from a priori definitions of humanity.

The quote above helps to explain my understanding of democracy's entanglements. It is unlikely that 'doing democracy' or 'being democratic' is solely for the domain of humans. Many of the animals we think do democratic things exist today. They existed before Homo sapiens evolved into what we are today. This point suggests interspecies learning or morality swapping along the evolutionary road. Democracy entanglement frees our thinking. It promotes the idea of looking to nonhumans that are exceptionally good at one or more democratic things and borrowing those tools for us to use. In short, EBD is not bound to humanity or comparative dichotomies.

EBD understands democracy as something that began rather simply around the dawn of life. Two billion years ago unicellular life forms were in the habit of cooperating, competing and communicating with kin and other species. They were able to act as autonomous agents but to also recognize groups. They could work as a group. Members of the same species were equal. Leadership changed frequently depending on who was releasing the chemical signals and what those signals meant. The only matter that held power over these cells was environmental. It dictated the behaviour of cells as these life forms adapted to survive under specific conditions. Humans can also be put under that condition: we depend on air, water, food and shelter. Without these environmental factors would we, could we, still be democrats?

This is a delicate discussion, and a tricky one too; biologists and physicists have as many doubts about the origins of life as political philosophers do about the origins of democracy. The ensuing discussions about nonhumans and why some species are democratic or anti-democratic, and sometimes both, is a work that operates from grave to grave.[1] We make best guesses based on the information available now. We depend on how we make sense out of this kind of information. The key is to be as capacious with our data as we can so as to make the best guesses humans can make at the present time. This is why we begin this chapter with an exploratory discussion.

Once a deeper introduction to the nonhuman evolutionary possibilities of democracy is complete, we will turn to discussing Boehm's (2012) *Ancestral Pan*. That discussion offers one story of how types of democracy manifested into the complexity we observe today (a discussion we pick up in Chapter 4). This finally leads to Chapter 3 where we offer arguments against the evolutionary perspective.

Particles, amino acids, microbes and sperm

The Australian theoretical physicist Austin Lund describes the use of 'democratic' and 'democracy' as terms in the physics literature as a slightly varied body. Although Democritus, 2,400 years ago, was one of the first individuals to discuss atoms there appears to be no explicit focus on democracy in physics. There is however a body of articles that discusses the collective governance of physics by physicists. But that literature is not what we are after. 'Democratic' and 'democracy' are used in different ways depending on the context of the article. Lund is our guide.

'Wrapping democracy' pertains to string theory. String theory is one of the theories used to describe high-energy experiments. It often requires the inclusion of all fundamental forces – things like spin and attraction. For wrapping experiments to be democratic the physicist must allow for the inclusion of all possible wrappings (membranes) and all possible intersections (where membranes meet). By including a wider number of variables in the study it becomes more inclusive; the study is forced to deal with a larger plurality of parameters; and this helps to ensure that there is balanced equality in the study before it is deployed. This is done to ensure that the user can make equally valid choices. The term 'democracy' connotes egalitarianism, equality and capaciousness. The same can be said for 'democratic mass matrix', 'democratic superstring field theory', 'democratic neutrinos' and 'flavor democracy'. Democracy in those works means egalitarianism.

In his explanation of wrapping in string theory, Lund brought up an interesting point. It has special importance for EBD. 'To match the low energy results that we have high confidence in, string theory must work in space-time dimensions larger than what we can experimentally see'. This is effectively reflected in what we are doing in this book. To prove the democracy results that we today have confidence in, democratic theory must work in space-time dimensions *larger* than what we can at this point experimentally see. That is an essential criterion of EBD. It helps to explain why the model I give in the Introduction focuses on time and space.

Itoh et al.'s (2001) use of 'democratic module PV system' is interesting. Their experiment ensures that the system has the same conditions for each variable that they are testing. They are looking for the best candidate from an equal field. Lund delivers poignantly with this remark: 'interestingly from their data there does not appear to be any particular candidate who is best under all conditions. Much like politics I guess' (in conversation, unpublished). Many of us would, I think, agree with that statement. This case, like the others looked at above, connotes the same starting point for all variables. The best performer is the one to focus on. That is an interesting understanding of democracy. It argues for agents to start under completely equal conditions and postulates that one or more agents will outperform the rest. A moral spin on this would be that agents under equal conditions should support *and* compete with each other to solve existing problems. That is possibly an ethos and telos for democracy out of physics or one put into physics.

The last and final physics and maths example we look at regards 'quantum democracy'. Segre (2010), a physicist who uses those terms, depends

DOI: 10.1057/9781137338662

on the US-American economist Kenneth Arrow's impossibility theorem. This theorem, which is popular in voting and electoral studies, lists three criteria for fairness in voting systems. It argues that no rank-order voting system can process communal preferences if there are three or more options given to voters *and* if the voting system must meet certain criteria. The criteria in this case relates to Arrow's conception of fairness. Physicists use the paradox because preferences, conditions and 'voting' can play a role in the evolution of their theories and experiments.

What Segre did was argue that a broader set of voting processes and a broader set of democratic conditions might resolve Arrow's paradox. It is one possible way of making quantum democracy. The finding is fascinating because it suggests that the answers to some of our current problems come from embracing complexity and not shying away from it. It argues that physicists, economists and political scientists need to be more capacious with the conditions of their studies when trying to provide answers that will hold true for a vast plurality of agents. We, humans, need to be more inclusive and cleverer. When trying to understand the big picture of the natural world or the phenomena of humanity we need to be able to work with greater complexity – and understand it. Otherwise, answering these big questions becomes improbable if not impossible.

On the one hand this discussion promotes the idea that the natural world, with all of its forces and particles together, make things happen in a big cooperative way. On the other hand it demonstrates that it is the physicist who places his or her own understanding of democratic conditions on the study. And on the third hand (why only have two?), the discussion shows that what we think is democracy or democratic has utility not only for humans but for how we understand the natural world.

The Chinese physicist Zhi-zhong Xing explains that 'democracy' and 'democratic' are used in relation to neutrinos, leptons and quarks. Physicists do this to manipulate their proofs to ensure that particles are even to each other. The explanation matches with what Lund says. This use of 'democracy' and 'democratic' has importance for a number of studies where particles need to be equal. That helps to explain why 'quantum democracy' is used as a term: it is possible to make a quantum field of particles identical by placing conditions here or there in the proof.

What Xing's insight tells us is that physicists understand democracy as a place where agents are made equal. It was in the 1980s that the Swedish

DOI: 10.1057/9781137338662

physicist Cecilia Jarlskog first proposed making particles equal. She borrowed the method Sweden used in progressive taxation to try to keep the net income of its citizens equal. The approach to personal income in Sweden, a part of its approach to democracy, is responsible for helping to create a new tool for the sciences. It does not mean that particles of any sort behave democratically which reinforces Lund's argument.

But current theory from astrobiology postulates that prebiotics are precursors to amino acids. And amino acids among numerous other types of molecules are central actors in the spontaneous formation of life. Woese (1998) argues that all life might come from a Last Universal Common Ancestor (LUCA) which is a hypothesis supported by the comparative phylogenetic analysis of ribonucleic acid (RNA). This suggests that both prebiotics and amino acids are central to any theory on democracy's evolution. How did LUCA come alive? What was the process like between prebiotics, aminos and the other building blocks involved? I am curious to know whether molecules communicate with each other, why they form more complex structures, and how they go about doing this. Is a democratic process involved with the formation of life itself?

The German physico–chemist Uwe Meierhenrich (2008), who is one of the individuals responsible for the discovery of amino acids in outer space, offers some answers. His work details the behaviour of molecules as they form into objects of greater complexity. Below I present a short interview that I had with him:

> **Gagnon:** What is a prebiotic in your work and how does it build amino acids? How then do amino acids lead to the creation of life and LUCA?
>
> **Meierhenrich:** We try to simulate the physico-chemical conditions that are observed in outer space, the so-called interstellar space. From spectroscopic observations we know that simple molecules such as H_2O [water], CO [carbon], CO_2 [carbon dioxide], MeOH [methanol] and NH_3 [ammonia] well occur in the gas phase in interstellar space. It is assumed that these molecules condense under interstellar conditions on dust particles while they are irradiated by interstellar and cosmic radiation. We simulate these processes in our laboratory. Under high vacuum we condense simple molecules on cold surfaces while irradiating with electromagnetic radiation; these conditions are very similar to conditions in interstellar space. Under such conditions we observe – somehow surprisingly – the formation of amino acids. Until today we have been able to identify 26 different amino acids. Some of them occur in proteins; others do not.

We assume that amino acids, once formed under interstellar conditions, condense to dimers and trimers [molecular building blocks] in suitable environments. Amino acids will further form oligomers, peptides, and eventually proteins. For these condensation steps, liquid water is probably required as well as the support of mineral surfaces. These surfaces are where the amino acids can adsorb and form peptide bonds to other amino acids in their local vicinity. These conditions are not yet established in detail in the laboratory and subject to intense (and fascinating) scientific debates.

Gagnon: I understand that there is a great complexity of molecular agents during the early stages of life creation: amino acids and sugar molecules have surprising asymmetrical qualities due to chirality [molecular orientation]. How do these different molecules go about working together? More importantly, why do they work together?

Meierhenrich: In the early stages of life creation we assume indeed a great complexity of molecules. Very different types of molecules occur in what some people call a 'prebiotic soup'. Also asymmetric (chiral) molecules occur in this soup and these molecules are assumed to occur in their left-handed as well as in their right-handed form. It is remarkable to note that proteins contain exclusively 'left-handed' amino acids, whereas 'right-handed' amino acids are not used for the biomolecular architecture of proteins. So if we imagine that a helix forms which is just by chance composed of some 'left-handed' amino acid molecules, this helix can continue to grow by adding left amino acids. Once a wrong, 'right-handed' amino acid is added, the growth of this oligomer immediately stops. In scientific language this phenomenon is called 'enantiomeric cross inhibition'. The wrong enantiomer inhibits the growth of the amino acid chain. The reason for this phenomenon is that a helix composed of left amino acids stabilizes itself, a helix composed of left and right amino acids is less stable. So the amino acids work together by constructing a stable molecule (the alpha helix). The formation of instable, labile reaction products is not favored.

Gagnon: Given your last answer, is it possible to argue that prebiotics and amino acids behave in 'democratic' ways when they are forming life? Are they communicating, is there decision-making, social learning, types of interchangeable leadership, altruistic behaviour by individuals for the common good, or phenomena similar to this?

Meierhenrich: I hesitate to call the behavior of amino acids 'democratic'. During the molecular origins of life, the amino acids follow rules that seem entirely imposed by thermodynamics and chemical kinetics. Stable products are formed; unstable products are less formed. Reactions showing high rate constants are favored over reactions with low rate constants. We should

DOI: 10.1057/9781137338662

think about the question of whether thermodynamics and kinetics can give rise to molecular behavior that might be called 'democratic'. The words 'self-assembled' or 'self-organized' are often used in a scientific context on specific arrangements of molecules. To my point of view these words do well describe the behavior of some molecules in certain environments.

Gagnon: Let us move a little bit out of this world. Given that aminos and prebiotics are found in objects from space and are hypothesized to be present in moon rocks and Martian materials, could we make the argument that certain 'democratic' things are occurring on meteorites, distant planets, and the universe at large?

Meierhenrich: Again, I agree that self-organizing molecules (such as amphiphilic molecules) are present in samples of meteorites. These molecules can form larger structures such as vesicles and liposomes. These amphiphilic molecules arrange themselves under specific conditions, such as pH values.

This auto-organization is due to the fact that external, mostly electrostatic interactions force each amphiphilic molecule to orient in space. Please note that it is not the individual molecule that 'decides' to orient. There is neither a choice for the molecule nor a decision to make. External physicochemical forces drive the orientation of molecules. If a set of molecules is concerned, we call this 'auto-organization'; I do not see a reason to call this comportment 'democratic'.

The interview reveals important things for democracy. Particles cannot make a decision because there is no decision to make. For life to occur, however, there must be success in how a plurality of particles cooperate and self-organize under specific conditions. We have to remember that this is an unimaginably gargantuan process of trial and error. As Meierhenrich reveals, particle chains can often form nothing if one molecule happens to go into the wrong place in a helix. It is up to chance then for particles, under the right conditions, to successfully form into chains and continuously build up into a mass capable of coming to life.

The spark between the inanimate and animate which leads to types of behaviour in the most basic forms of life is where the focus of future study should be directed. When does a mass of molecules suddenly become a cell? And when did this cell decide to undergo mitosis, swap genetics, sense chemical signals and all the rest of it? How did this lead to us with our big brains, morals and self-awareness? To me it seems that these things just happened. I think inanimate matter came to life in an unimaginable amount of times over 13 billion years in the known

DOI: 10.1057/9781137338662

universe. In some places like earth these sparks led to phenomena like mitosis. These hardy cells endured harsh conditions. Or they died and new ones emerged. What this discussion suggests is that democratic ways of existing were most likely created by chance with the many LUCAs during the dawns of life itself. Democratic phenomena have been evolving for billions of years and, just like their numerous antitheses, they are a collection of techniques among many for the propagation of life.

Humans, us moral creatures, and other possibly moral animals, decide to behave as democrats. We do not want to be violent autocrats because we value things we are in the habit of calling democratic ideals. Examples of the tension between both extremes are endemic to the history of humanity. Our conscious decision to focus on democracy, to be democrats, and to democratize is a step in the evolution of our species. We only have to figure out what we mean by it.

Evidence from the sciences continues as we scale to slightly more complicated forms of life. Sperm cells are an interesting case. Millions of individuals are in development together within the testes and are released together in the ejaculation. The behaviour of these many gametes changes depending on the species we look at. Böhmer et al. (2005) shows that chemotaxis (the ability to detect chemical signalling) is used by sperm to find one or more eggs. Kaupp et al. (2008) show that each individual has photoreceptors and olfactory neurons: sperm can 'see' and 'smell' to some extent. Sperm cooperate and compete with each other. They are thought to be capable of rapidly evolving in response to changes in their environment (Schärer et al., 2011). One type of sperm from deer mice has the capacity to recognize their genetic kin (in the case of multiple mating by a female with several males) and form 'trains to speed up their passage to the egg' (Fisher and Hoekstra, 2010: 801).

> Among the extraordinary adaptations driven by sperm competition is the cooperative behaviour of spermatozoa. By forming cooperative groups, sperm can increase their swimming velocity and thereby gain an advantage in intermale sperm competition.

These cooperating 'brother' sperm also have the ability to decide to 'prematurely trigger the reaction that is used to bore through the egg's wall. This speeds the train on its way, but amounts to suicide for the sperm that triggered the reaction' (Whitman, 2010). Oxford University's Kevin Foster, professor of evolutionary biology, says that the gametes involved in these trains enter a fair lottery. When triggering the bore reaction,

DOI: 10.1057/9781137338662

the average payout is greater than the average cost as each gamete has, under current understandings, an equal chance of joining with the egg. In certain systems some sperm have a better chance at fertilizing the egg than others due to slight genetic superiority. Biologists are uncertain over whether sperm have any agency – they could be controlled by the male that released them. It seems, however, that there is a type of fairness between sperm.

Foster continues. Gametes offer another example of cooperation. Individuals enact a process that biologists call meiosis. This is gene recombination that occurs between individual gametes. Current thinking shows that meiosis happens for gene repair, making new genetic combinations to deal with changing environments (particularly to avoid parasites), and breaking up self-interested gene combinations. What we do not know is whether this meiosis is a forced behaviour or whether it is emblematic of some basic system of autonomous agents.

The study of how gametes interact with each other is a nascent field. Some observations allow us to argue that gametes behave in certain, specific democratic ways. We know that there is fierce but non-violent competition and that there is also cooperation. If gametes can in theory or observation be argued to have ongoing types of democratic behaviour this will support the notion that democracy can be based on both competition and cooperation: not simply one or the other.

Just as we saw at the end of Chapter 1 similar arguments are being made about bacteria.

> Microbes have traditionally been thought of as free-living individual (selfish) organisms that display little group identity and group behavior. Viruses of microbes are even less thought of in the context of a role in group identity. However, we have recently come to realize that our world is predominantly prokaryotic, such as seen with the most visible example of life from space: blooms of cyanobacteria ... We have also come to realize that this prokaryotic world is itself often communal (living in blooms, mats, biofilms) and that group behaviors are also prevalent. Prokaryotes thus provide the beginnings of molecular systems that regulate group identity. (Villareal, 2009: 27)

This discussion of particles, prebiotics and sperm is a heuristic designed to shine the light on the possible origins of democracy itself. What it helps to do is establish the possibility of an evolutionary origin to democracy – similar to what has been proposed about the origins of violence and cooperation. It shows that EBD takes a *very* broad focus on time and space. But the discussion we had in the first half of this chapter represents a body of unknown literature. There is a more established, still little known, body of works about more complex nonhumans. It is to these we now turn to.

Bonobos, mole rats, slime-moulds and crows

The bonobo is an animal sometimes called 'the forgotten ape'. And we do not know as much about them as we do, for example, about chimpanzees. Biologists consider bonobos more social and less violent than chimpanzees. Bonobo females frequently interact with each other. For the most part, males do not kill each other over females. And intergroup conflict is moderate (Furuichi, 2011). Certain chimpanzee societies on the other hand tend to suffer from violent males, less social females, cases of infanticide, rape and murder during intergroup relations. Sometimes murder or rape occurs within the group. Both bonobos and chimpanzees behave in their own democratic ways. In the case of chimps, their violent streak suppresses the dimensions of democracy. Still, biologists focus on chimpanzees because of their cooperative hunting, tool use, politics, self-awareness and ability to wage types of war (Waal, 1995). These are human traits but mostly not democratic traits. Humans are suggested to have split from the bonobo/chimpanzee common ancestor some 5 to 8 million years ago (Waal, 1995; Roach, 2011).

Certain chimp societies living in western parts of Africa behave differently to chimps in the east. Where there are no gorillas to compete with for food, and more bountiful resources, chimps tend to behave more like bonobos (Roach, 2011). This suggests that resource scarcity is, at least for chimps, a determiner of their political behaviour. During the tough times, survival depends on being violent. For bonobos survival depends on females sticking together and pushing males to the periphery. Bonobos deal with food scarcity by forming smaller groups to forage until abundance returns. Conflicts for bonobos are frequent but are usually settled through vocalizations and sex – although sometimes through violence. Chimpanzees seem to settle conflicts mostly through violence and male domination although alpha females sometimes act as intermediaries during intragroup conflict.

Bonobos are remarkable because of their peaceful type of existence. This is why we focus on them in this chapter. Waal (1995: 82) shares that bonobos have egalitarian and female-centred societies. Bonobos usually use communication and brief sex instead of violence to settle the many disputes that arise in their societies. They are also in the habit of soothing upset individuals until the problem dissipates.

> Although selecting the chimpanzee as the touchstone of hominid evolution represented a great improvement [the former focus was on baboons], at least one aspect of the former model did not need to be revised: male superiority remained the natural state of affairs. In both baboons and chimpanzees, males are conspicuously dominant over females; they reign supremely and often brutally. It is highly unusual for a fully grown male chimpanzee to be dominated by any female. (Waal, 1995: 82)

> For decades, scenarios of human evolution have depicted our ancestors as 'killer apes,' progressing from aggression to hunting and warfare. While work on some monkeys and apes (notably baboons and chimpanzees) supported this view, studies of the most recently recognized ape species, the bonobo, both in the wild and in captivity, certainly do not. (Waal, 1997: 22)

Bonobos challenge previous assumptions that our nearest ancestors were male-centric and naturally violent or oppressive. They communicate using facial expressions, body-language and various high-pitch sounds. Humans have numerous ways of settling conflicts, and chimpanzees do too. But bonobos are in the habit of using sexual acts to diffuse tension, reaffirm the group's social fabric and reconcile after disputes. If two males for example happen to fight over mating with a female, they eventually return to hug each other. This, some biologists say, is sometimes accompanied by kissing. Mutual scrotal rubbing and masturbation are observed phenomena. Females also use mutual genital rubbing for reconciliation.

Although the point has some contention to it, the bulk of biologists seem to favour the view that violence and warfare are improbable with bonobos. Aggressive behaviour is still present but restrained. Two males in conflict communicate without interrupting one another (Waal, 1997: 25). Individuals, usually females, can leave their natal group when encountering a different group and possibly join them. The apes are today renowned for their achievements in peaceful conflict resolution and sensitivity to others (Waal, 1997).

> Just imagine that we had never heard of chimpanzees or baboons and had known bonobos first. We would at present most likely believe that early hominids lived in female-centered societies, in which sex served important

DOI: 10.1057/9781137338662

> social functions and in which warfare was rare or absent. In the end, perhaps the most successful reconstruction of our past will be based not on chimpanzees or even on bonobos but on a three-way comparison of chimpanzees, bonobos and humans. (Waal, 1995: 88).

US-American social anthropologist Christopher Boehm (2012) argues that comparing humans, bonobos and chimpanzees is useful. It helps to understand how humans became moral beings. We are able to make conscious decisions. The bonobos appear morally favourable to democrats – certain chimpanzees less so. Both species, our cousins, highlight that we were never predestined for anything. The decisions made by certain humans in specific times and places led to more democracy or less democracy. We are a mixture of both with the capacity for acting like both. Today we value peace over violence, sharing over selfishness and altruism over deceit. We are collectively evolving.

We gain further insight by moving down in animal size to more distant relatives. Mole rats, of which there are various kinds, live in underground tunnel systems. Two types (naked mole rats and Damaraland mole rats) are eusocial.[2] They labour, digging tunnels in search of tubers, insects and other roots 'for the good of the colony' (Milius, 2006). Workers carry food back to a communal repository. These mole rats communicate using more than 16 vocalizations. They have communal toilets which, when full, eventually become blocked by purposefully built walls. New toilet rooms are then dug. They redigest their own faeces for vitamin D and offer faeces to the queen when she is pregnant and cannot redigest her own. There are even 'couch-potato' males in the colony who do little work during arid periods and eat the food brought back by others.

Mole rats behave in this eusocial way because of the harsh conditions they live in. They must cooperate for survival (Bennett and Faulkes, 2000). The freeloading males are thought to store fat for the rainy season. After the rains, which soften the soil, these males frantically dig tunnels in the hopes of finding a different colony or female to mate with. This practice is seen in honeybees too. Drones, or male bees, will lounge about begging food off their sisters. They then use this energy to fly around looking for a queen to mate with: drones are essentially flying penises. These 'lazy' males are needed to dash off from the family and promote genetic diversity by breeding with a female from a different family, or, in the case of mole rats, get eaten by a snake. This is apparently a common occurrence.

DOI: 10.1057/9781137338662

That being said, mole rats are dominated by a queen. Their society is hierarchical. Bigger rats have more status than smaller rats (Yosida and Okanoya, 2009). Without a queen females will fight violently to murder each other until one dominant female has emerged triumphant. This type of sororicide is seen in bees and wasps too. For mole rats, the queen walks over other rats (instead of sliding past them which is the usual custom between rats) and at times charges another individual's nose with her own as if to put that individual in their place. Despite the eusociality of these animals they are not able to make decisions collectively. They are biologically driven to make the colony work which is what bees, ants, termites, wasps and other insects and mammals do. Can we argue then that a type of democracy is present in mole rat society?

The only escape for an individual mole rat is to wall themselves off from the colony. The individual does this in the hopes of reaching another lone individual of the opposite sex with which they might begin their own colony and rule over their own offspring. I would say that although the mole rats communicate and work for the greater good, they are not a democracy. They do certain democratic things well but the system they evolved is a form of monarchy or a type of suppressed democracy. The queen does not hold council. Larger mole rats do not act as elites checking centralized power.

Now slime mould, the social amoeba, is another nonhuman entity that has 'democratic' traits. There are over one hundred slime mould species, each with different behaviours. This creature is a cross between an animal and a fungus. It thrives in moist, warm, soil covered with dead leaves and other edible things like dung. It feeds on bacteria and other amebae (Waddell and Vogel, 1985). Although slime moulds share more genes with animals than they do with other fungi, they have no central nervous system. Slime moulds reproduce using spores. Once a spore (basically a flying amoeba) lands on a food source it emerges to feed as a unicellular body. For larger species this body travels at about 1 cm per hour in search for more food. Smaller species tend not to travel. Once the food is eaten, this cell communicates with nearby cells which then come together to form a larger multicellular body. This body, which looks like a small slug, travels to the surface of the soil. It reorganizes its cells and becomes a type of mushroom-looking stalk. It induces spore formation. The slime mould eventually releases another round of flying amoeba that float to other places and the process begins once more.

DOI: 10.1057/9781137338662

It is important to know that some slime mould biologists argue certain species to have evolved cheating mechanisms. Certain cells have evolved a trait that denies other cells from moving past the stalk-forming stage. Some call this cheating. Others are calling this altruistic behaviour on the part of the cells that form the stalk. Without those stalk cells that eventually die the propagation of their species would not be possible. It is another example of cooperation and competition at the same time. Both are effective and needed in this case to achieve the telos of the slime mould: successful propagation.

Slime moulds have a type of intelligence. If cut up into pieces and scattered in a maze that has food in the middle the creature knows how to unite itself and navigate the maze. It finds the food and begins eating it (Nakagaki, 2001). Slime moulds travel upwards from beneath the soil to the surface. They can recognize light, temperature and types of gas (the difference between oxygen, an attractant, and ammonia, a repellent). When cells unite for migratory purposes we call them 'slugs' (Bonner and Lamont, 2005). When they reach the surface and begin their reproductive cycle we call them 'stalks'. Certain slime moulds practice bacteria husbandry. They effectively farm bacteria and carry them as a portable food source during stalk formation (Boomsma, 2011).

These creatures are capable of coordinated movement and organized behaviour between different amoebas. That is why I include them in this chapter. Amoebas work together. During favourable conditions each individual cell wanders its own way eating its preferred food. But when conditions worsen, the cells release a type of chemical which signals others to band together (Nishikawa et al., 2005). It is collective action with no recognizable ruler. Communal consciousness drives survival. Evolution in response to the forces of nature might be the ruler in this sense. This unicellular life form cooperates with others to propagate their species. Bozzone (1997: 565) tells that certain slime mould species eat different foods so as not to be direct competitors. This is a type of inter-species cooperation or niche-sharing.

Crows are the final and briefest example that we look at before moving onto the next chapter. Izawa (2008) calls these birds 'feathered primates' due to their social structures. He argues that Jungle Crows can identify other individuals, what they are doing and then use this social structure which changes throughout the day or activity to the bird's own advantage (Izawa, 2007). Crows, like other corvids (i.e. magpies and jays), are able to learn from one another. In an experiment that involves

DOI: 10.1057/9781137338662

trapping several crows and banding them while wearing a specific mask, researchers documented how those crows captured, and those crows watching the capture, communicated to others about who the dangerous human is. Parents taught their juveniles and adults learned from other adults about the bad mask. Those crows captured were better able to distinguish between neutral masks and the bad mask. Crows transmitted this information over approximately 1.2 kilometres. The communal memory of the crows about this bad mask lasted five years for one test site (Cornell et al., 2011).

Crows have a habit of foraging for food socially. They sometimes do this using tools. While migrating to wintering grounds, American crows land where other crows are foraging as this suggests that food is available (Ward and Raim, 2011). They can even differentiate between familiar and unfamiliar human and jackdaw voices (Wascher et al. 2012) which aids corvids in identifying potentially useful individuals in multi-species flocks.

The four examples of nonhuman 'democratic' societies that I draw on above establish certain points. Nonhumans have evolved practices and behaviours that are dependent on their environments. Humans consider these practices to be 'democratic'. The list below shows the 'democratic' traits that we discuss in this chapter. The list relates well to the more complex of the nonhumans:

- cooperation;
- conflict resolution;
- sensitivity to others;
- communication;
- social learning;
- coordination;
- communal behaviour;
- self-awareness (this is important for sensing environmental changes);
- awareness of kin and non-kin from the same species;
- and awareness of, if not communication with, individuals from different species.

The items listed above are used by animals to ensure their survival. Biologists argue that these democratic behaviours increase fitness – or the likelihood of one or more animals surviving. We think the teleology of social animals is to achieve successful reproduction. In that logic, democratic behaviours are central for the survival of species. Recalling

DOI: 10.1057/9781137338662

Table 1.1, that survey of nonhumans demonstrates that these survival techniques are common. Different basic democratic behaviours are useful for nonhumans: even certain chimpanzees get out of violent power politics when the times are good.

What we also learn from these nonhumans is that most cannot decide how their democracies will manifest. Mole rats, ants and bees are stuck in evolutionary determinism due to their limited cognitive abilities. Humans can decide whether they will be peaceful or violent. We decide whether we will work alone or together. We manipulate the ways in which we communicate. We can cooperate or dominate. Democratic behaviours and their antitheses are observable in nature. They are observable in humans.

The point I make here concerns the list of nonhuman democratic traits. To me it seems that the first seven items are normative desires in human societies across a broad swathe of planetary time and space. This is why Seeley (2011, 2013) argues that humans can learn from the effective decision-making of bees. Or why Waal states that we can make moral judgements about our own behaviour by contrasting bonobos and chimpanzees. Humans evolved with democracy and autocracy but I think there was always the underlying will to work in democratic ways – the way that many nonhumans do because cooperation brings more benefits to the individual. No dominant single individual can provide what communal governance gives. The argument that humans are predisposed to democracy and to the constant resistance to violence and domination is one that is supported by nonhuman evidence.

Ancestral Pan and the complexity of democracy

Boehm's concept of the Ancestral Pan species, or the animal that existed before humans branched off from bonobos and chimpanzees, has basic behaviour. Ancestral Pan had male and female mediators during conflicts. They were able to create agreements within the group and with other groups to reduce violence. And they lived in egalitarian bands where leadership rotated frequently – possibly on a moment to moment basis. Our ancestors were careful to deny the type of political escalation that occurs primarily during alpha-male competition: it is injurious to the greater good and should be avoided. But these systems sometimes failed. Some bands were violent, some individuals inconsolable and

DOI: 10.1057/9781137338662

some alpha-males too strong. Peace between bands sometimes could not happen. Individuals may have murdered each other in fits of rage, jealousy or through similar motives.

I think this helps to explain how and why different democracies sprang as humans continued to grow in numbers, spread over more spaces and evolve. Tensions between peace and violence existed for us over millions of years. Different conditions forced different innovations. Climate change, population increases, technological innovations, arms scaling, empire building, ideological domination, kin over community (Fukuyama, 2011), promoting the self at the expense of others, and different types of domination forced subalterns, injured peers and moralistic elites to make changes to their societies and to themselves.

Pathos, our emotions, is an interesting indicator for natural inclinations to democracy. I suspect that there will be an increasingly long list of phenomena across planetary space and time where humans are found to have behaved in democratic ways. More evidence will show where humans worked together to resist domination and where humans made democracies for themselves. These things decayed, were voted into suicide or were sublimated by irresistible forces. It appears to me as a pendulum: swinging from one side to another across time, space and species. Are we today capable of breaking out of this pattern? Can we hold the pendulum to the democratic side to deny its movements to the other?

Notes

1 This phrase comes from a discussion with the theoretical physicist Omri Bahat Treidel.

2 Eusociality has various definitions. Here, in this chapter, it means a society uses a number of cooperative techniques to propagate its species.

DOI: 10.1057/9781137338662

3
Arguments against Evolutionary Democracy

Abstract: *This chapter is best understood as a tale of two stories. The first half describes the type of foundational claim that places the origins of 'modern' democracy during the period of North Atlantic revolutions. Although a nod is given to ancient Athens it is not viewed as a legitimate democracy but rather a source of ideas for moderns to draw on. The second half of the chapter describes the arguments that see democracy on the horizon. The government and governance we call democracy has not yet arrived. And if it has, it has done so only in part. It must improve to be more democratic. The chapter demonstrates the contestability of democracy's origins and the anthropocentrism inherent in dominant understandings of democracy.*

Gagnon, Jean-Paul. *Evolutionary Basic Democracy: A Critical Overture*, Basingstoke: Palgrave Macmillan, 2013.
DOI: 10.1057/9781137338662.

This chapter demonstrates that democracy's dominant narratives are inescapably human. For all but one example, nonhumans have no role in the two narratives that we are going to look at. The first narrative takes the revolutionary periods of the North Atlantic as the place of modern democracy's origins. Parts of democratic Hellas, usually ancient Athens, gets a nod in this literature. But this nod is used to designate where certain ideas came from and how philosophers like Edmund Burke, Alexis de Tocqueville, Tom Paine and John Stuart Mill came to elaborate on them.

> Modern democracy, while rooted in the ancient civilizations of Greece and Rome, was propelled by the players, beliefs, and events of Europe in the 18th, 19th, and 20th centuries. Grounded by enlightenment optimism about progress, liberty, and human rights, modern Europeans reinvented their political, economic, and social institutions to reflect these new ideals. Indeed, they waged battle for these beliefs through a series of revolutions that would transform daily life and expectations for every social class. (Campbell, 2011: xi)

Although ancient Athens was erroneously thought to have been the first democracy it was not a model for modernity. Something new was needed. During the centuries leading up to the revolutions of the 1700s, the assembly typology promoting the participation of a type of 'common man' was distasteful for aristocrats and aspiring elites. Moral and logical wars ensued in Europe. These were inspired by the Greek and Romans and medieval lore. These recollections of shared experience culminated in triumphant revolutions that established democracy once and for all. This is the way that many speak of the rise of democracy itself. What this story does tell is *one version* of the evolution of a *type* of democracy for a *specific* set of times and spaces. It is not the story of humanity's democracy.

The second narrative that we look at establishes the origins of democracy elsewhere. This literature recurrently nods to assembly and representative types of democracy – but scoffs at them too. How can Cleisthenic Athens or Paris in 1790 be considered democracies if their citizenries were limited, the franchise miniscule and violence widespread? Scholars that look to ancient democracies circumvent these critiques by stating 'those were the times'. They then move to analysing ancient and impressive institutions. There are numerous theories, concepts and practices of democracy, each with their own moral ethos, that argue for the things that need to come. 'For democracy to exist we need to implement this thing' and 'for democracy to exist we need to broaden

DOI: 10.1057/9781137338662

that parameter'. I view this heuristic as 'democracy on the horizon'. These types of arguments keep us looking forward. Democracy is coming. The lady can be seen standing in the prow of her ever-nearing boat. We hope that she lands on our sometimes wretched shores. We worry that she might never land and remain, as some have said, only visible through the magnifying effect of a looking glass.

I think that it is clear at this juncture in the book that evolutionary basic democracy (EBD) views democracy as a phenomenon, one that stretches across vast times and spaces. What I demonstrate in this chapter is that EBD's wholesome look is unusual. The discourse of democracy has been colonized by Eurocentric and then US-American empire. It remains dominated by certain times and places. Democracy is also stuck in a morass of contemporary uncertainties which negatively affects current politics. The root of these problems is our uncertainty over what democracy for *all* humanity means. We have not been able to provide a definition that works across all of time and space. Lady democracy might disembark, but only if we can provide her with a scientific foundation to step on. That foundation is something, as I argued in the Introduction, that does not exist.

Democracy born in revolution

There is no easy-to-define body of literature that specifically argues against evolutionary narratives. Rather, these kinds of arguments are dispersed across the literature. Logic dictates that if a foundational claim on democracy is being made in recent history it disqualifies previous claims. In this view, older democracies were preludes to democracy. They were something else.

The Introduction and Chapter 1 discussed the Grecian debates on democracy's origin. These debates explain why this foundational claim is wrong. This first half of Chapter 3 looks at claims founding democracy in the historical North Atlantic. It is in these times and places that modern democracy was born. Some argue that this is the only relevant foundation of democracy for contemporary times. Arguments from Wood (1969) and Campbell (2011), for example, place the birth of modern democracy with the US and French revolutions. Others see modern democracy as a product of the English revolution.

I take the French Revolution as a case study. But the US, English or Russian revolutions would work equally well. Some consider the French

DOI: 10.1057/9781137338662

Revolution to be the 'triumph of man'. For American political scientist Francis Fukuyama, by way of the German philosopher G. W. F. Hegel and others, it was the Battle of Jena where the ideals of the French Revolution gained dominance in the early 1800s. It was a change of the old guard, a triumph of the many over the privileged few. It was the victory of modern democracy that the past two centuries have only come to build upon.

Weitman (1968) takes a unique approach regarding the French foundations of democracy. Instead of claiming that the French Revolution posed as the cradle for later European democracies, or democracy itself in modernity, he asks why the Revolution turned toward democracy at all. Why not something else? One answer is probably because there were no other alternatives that had weight in the moral philosophies leading up to the revolution. Indeed, in our contemporary literature, democracy is considered to have no alternatives. Whatever it is, it is the best we have.

Commentators during and after the French Revolution recognize that some achievements were made among its terror, violence and deaths. Ideas in social, political and economic ideology were fermenting in the 1700s. Monarchs, the Catholic Church, and certain aristocrats, protected businesses, as well as military structures came under increasing ethical pressure from both elites and non-elites. Governing in the interest of the elite and a disdain for 'the common man' became increasingly perceived as fundamental injustices.

Parts of France in the 1790s and early 1800s underwent a series of policy shifts. Changes were made to what a democratic citizenry means. It was a place of innovation. It was also a place of danger. The guillotine is one reminder. French beginnings contrasted with English beginnings. The foundational narrative during the time of North Atlantic revolutions is not homogeneous. Anglo-American liberal democracy is not the dominant model of democracy for modernity. The French or European approach is its rival. We have to, however, be careful with these kinds of explanations because both the Anglo-American and French-European approaches are subjective. It comes down to how an individual explains each camp and, specifically, how this individual contrasts the two.

Bourke (2008: 10) explains why the French Revolution, or its cognates, is argued to be a starting point for modern democracy:

> Modern conceptions of democracy are for the most part static. Very often they are ideologically programmatic too. There is a connection between these two aspects of democratic theory. Static conceptions can serve the

> purpose of ideological definition by the very fact of their agreeable simplicity: they offer a snapshot – a frozen analysis – shorn of disagreeable complications. This kind of static analysis is a reversion to the earliest modes of political description in the Western tradition.

The 'why' of the foundation is clear: the revolution destroyed parts of an increasingly unethical and unjust monarchy. Ensuing battles on pitch or paper imbued certain ideals with more power. The elites of old fell. 'Common man' rose and a new system of elites gained footing. Women, children, nature, religious and ethnic minorities, and other subalterns were excluded. Many suffered. It is a story of a nexus point. Something called democracy began with the French Revolution. But what exactly came out of the Battle of Jena or its cognates? How did the ideals that drove the revolution cement themselves under its authoritarian and brutally violent aftermath? Wollstonecraft (1795) suggests that it was the people throughout France and those outside of this State. They knew of the ideals and of the violence that robbed them of their chance for flourishing in pluralist society. It was these people that protected the flame of democratic principles that burned on a delicate wick.

Fukuyama argues that the Napoleonic victory over monarchic Prussia in 1806 solidified the principles of equality and liberty. But the meaning of the two terms was fiercely debated during the revolutionary period. Perhaps what the Battle of Jena did was solidify a commitment to these vague ideals. States, after Jena, would not be able to work against the two principles. If they did, they would be held in contempt by those individuals that feel unequal. And by those individuals whose liberty is trodden on. The Battle of Jena was indeed a momentous occasion for *parts* of Europe. It helped to create awareness of certain principles that many hold dear for democracy. It empowered non-elites. And it emboldened resistance against most, if not all, forms of tyranny. The State, males, the Church, greedy bosses, aristocratic arses, and others of that vein became increasingly aware of the common person's reproachful eye.

John Adams (the second president of the United States) had said, after the onset of revolutions and uprisings in the early 1800s, that he did not intend for this outcome when framing the constitution of the USA. He felt that it was the US–American revolution that acted as the watershed of democracy. It was responsible for inspiring the French Revolution and the subsequent revolts in many parts of Western Europe. I think he meant that he was sorry for the violence that came out of these revolutions and resistance movements. I am uncertain whether he lamented the fall of reproachful institutions or individuals.

A useful story of how the foundational claim of the French Revolution produced different interpretations comes from Irish philosopher Edmund Burke and British philosopher Mary Wollstonecraft (O'Neill, 2007). We will contrast their positions on the revolution with the actions of Nicolas de Condorcet (Marie Jean Antoine Nicolas de Caritat, Marquis de Condorcet). This discussion helps to highlight the subjectivity of foundational claims to democracy in the revolutionary period – and any other period. Burke (1790) begins his description of the revolution in his letters and then in a more coherent position that he elucidates in the book *Further Reflections on the French Revolution*. The sentiments of liberty and equality were brewing in the hearts and minds of many French individuals leading up to their revolution. These were not different to the ones that English persons held in the middle and then later 1600s. The French, Burke argued, reacted too radically to what they viewed as the abhorrent excesses of the monarchy. And the monarchy acted pitiably when it fled Paris. Burke, in 1791, wanted to see an international coalition of monarchies against France. In short, it seems, the French seem to have done the revolution wrong. It produced Jacobins, terrorized much of the population and spread violence. The revolution should have been done gradually, in partnership with the monarchy, and in line with presumably 'English' sentiments.

Wollstonecraft (1795) approaches the revolution similarly. She argues that the French began something remarkable. It was a push by an enlightened majority of individuals to create a stable state, one based on the principles of the enlightenment such as the responsibility to protect the weak. It was a rebellion against 'unjust and cruel laws' (Wollstonecraft, 1795: 8). Despite the good intentions of an increasingly educated body of French citizens, it was violence that ruined their chances.

> The rapid changes, the violent, the base, and nefarious assassinations, which have clouded the vivid prospect that began to spread a ray of joy and gladness over the gloomy horizon of oppression, cannot fail to chill the sympathizing bosom, and palsy intellectual vigour. To sketch these vicissitudes is a task so arduous and melancholy, that, with a heart trembling to the touches of nature, it becomes necessary to guard against the erroneous inferences of sensibility; and reason beaming on the grand theatre of political changes, can prove the only sure guide to direct us to a favourable or just conclusion. This important conclusion, involving the happiness and

> exaltation of the human character, demands serious and mature consideration; as it must ultimately sink the dignity of society into contempt, and its members into greater wretchedness; or elevate it to a degree of grandeur not hitherto anticipated, but by the most enlightened statesmen and philosophers. (Wollstonecraft, 1795: 6)

Condorcet (1795) shares the opinion with Wollstonecraft and Burke that the revolution was initially a triumph of enlightenment principles. Mathematical thinking, or logic, dealt superstitious ignorance a deathly blow. The empowerment of women was a growing reality. These points were agreed upon by the three thinkers. Condorcet was active in the politicking of the less violent period of the revolution. He seems to have entertained some toleration for proposed violence against the monarchy – a violent means to a democratic end? This was in stark contrast to Burke and Wollstonecraft who lamented and opposed violence of this sort. The historiography of Condorcet's political actions shows that he was firmly against the wider and looser violence that followed the Girondin's resistance to the Montagnards.[1] Despite Condorcet's intentions, the resulting belief in the revolution by the Jacobins and then Napoleon was that violence was a legitimate means for the imposition of democratic principles. Loyalists to monarchs, individuals intolerant of the violence that blind belief in radicalism spreads, monarchic states, and powerful aristocrats had to fall by sword or other means if democracy was to succeed. It is a different spin on this one foundational claim for modern democracy.

The approaches to explaining or understanding the revolution from Burke, Wollstonecraft and Condorcet establish three points. The first is that this one foundational claim of democracy is inescapably anthropocentric. Most foundational claims are. The second is that it is contested – there are numerous ways of explaining origination. Any other case study of democracy's origins has this type of contestation. Some, for example, say that the French Revolution is a more democratic one than the English or American. Others say that it is less. Certain individuals link the French Revolution to ancient Athens. Others do not link it at all. The third point is that a number of explanations for this origin of democracy are inextricably European. They disregard most of the data from other times and spaces. These three points, if taken together, argue against the idea of an evolutionary democracy. This thing, democracy, is the product of specific and brilliant inventions that happened in specific times and places. It is the product of specific individuals and their thoughts and

DOI: 10.1057/9781137338662

struggles. It is European. And it is something that an increasing number of thinkers heartily disagree with.

Democracy on the horizon

Despite the claims by others that democracy was born in Athens, France, the USA, England, the post-war ashes of Europe or elsewhere, there is a convincing counter-argument that deserves elucidation. It is the view that democracy has not yet arrived. Some might construct the discussion we will have below as the process of 'democracy arriving'. In this narrative, humans have made numerous efforts to establish democracy but have failed in each regard. The fact that we do not know what democracy is plays a role in this thinking too. Because its definitions are varied we must take into account its diverse past, its many current manifestations and combine these to form a teleology for us to reach. Democracy then could not have come from the principles won at the Battle of Jena or in the Straits of Salamis.[2] It is something that we are still building and trying to figure out.

Keane (2009), for example, argues about the future of monitory democracy. He describes this theory by differentiating it from assembly democracy and representative democracy. These previous forms of government and governance were efforts at democracy but could not achieve it due, in part, to their lack of accountability, transparency and anti-corruption. It was not common in ancient Athens or London in 1850 for the vast majority of individuals to participate in politics. Women and young property-less men had significant barriers to accessing politics. It was difficult to gain information about public taxes and to have much, if any, influence over who would represent you. The malaises of assembly and representative systems are well documented for contemporary times. Even though individuals are given a vote, it tends not to count for much. Even though constituencies are represented – it is not as if representation is wondrously effective.

From Keane's perspective, democracy can exist only if it has a diverse collection of individuals, associations, assemblies and representations. These criteria must be held in check by multiple universes[3] of monitorism. From governing the self to global government there has been a remarkable increase for what I call the 'new holy trinity': accountability, transparency and anti-corruption. This trinity, for example, extends to

DOI: 10.1057/9781137338662

media, business, public institutions, family life and university administration. The worry from Keane and others is that monitorism might be resisted by the enemies of democracy. That it will crumble in the face of elite opposition, the political and communal apathy of individuals, and the sober reality of how hard it is to achieve our collective aims. We are trying to innovate ways that will resolve the problems we have with assemblies and representation. We are trying to be better at monitorism. But will it be enough?

The British political theorist Carole Pateman and the now sadly late American political theorist Iris Marion Young argued, as early as the 1970s, that for democracy to exist it needs substantive participation. Over the past four decades arguments in this part of the literature state that the citizenry has to be much wider than it is. Recall that in the 1970s women throughout the 'west' still had not yet achieved the universal franchise; there were significant racist barriers for people of African, Latino and indigenous descent; and access to information from the government was much harder to come by. The point of entry into political voice for citizens has to extend past casting a ballot. Individuals and associations should have easier access to their representatives. And institutions need to operate on these principles of inclusion and participation. Wingenbach (2011) makes this point in his reconsideration of agonistic democratic theory. He argues that institutions should be founded on liberal agonism: a theory based on principles of capaciousness, inclusiveness, resistance and flexible foundations.

Pateman and Young's work lead to arguments about the inclusion and participation of youth as members of the citizenry. Can we have democracy where teenagers below 18 years of age are not permitted to cast a ballot? Children and teenagers do often play a role in politics. They can visit politicians, write to them, make collective decisions in student unions, be filmed in advocacy videos and be seen at political rallies. But despite this recognition they are still informal members of the citizenry. Should they not, like tourists and non-residents, be given greater voice through a vote and the right to run for election?

The Australian political theorist Robyn Eckersley also has interesting things to say about participation, representation and the citizenry. A growing discourse, termed critical political ecology, is making a number of interesting arguments. It asks poignant questions. The various foundational claims to democracy over the past two-and-a-half millennia are inescapably human. It is an assembly of people. Individual humans are represented. People form citizenries. But what about trees, streams and brooks? And animals, ecosystems and oceans? If humans are animals, and we depend on nonhuman things for our survival, then are we not representing them too in our politicking? That is an interesting point that emerged over the past 50 years of increasingly popular environmental politics. For democracy to exist we need to not only include the representation of nonhumans, but those humans that are too disabled to represent themselves, and those humans yet to be born many future generations from now.

Critical political ecology has seen practical manifestation in contemporary politics. In 2008, the Constitution of Ecuador gave legal rights to nature. It is a system of public law that gives enforceable rights to nonhumans. When a human feels that a forest, animal or river has had their rights violated, humans act as their legal *representatives.* This constitution is also celebrated for its enshrinement of human and nonhuman right to food. It raises a novel dimension of the rights that must be present if a democracy is to work: pure water, healthy food and clean air should be inviolable rights for any human and nonhuman.

Over the past 20 years greater focus on types of political participation has emerged. The emphasis is on how we can measure the quality of participation. Are there techniques that humans can use to improve the nature of collaboration, cooperation and communal decisions? Dryzek, Belgique democratic theorist Didier Caluwaerts and English democratic theorist Stephen Elstub argue that the third generation of deliberative or discursive democracy is that tool. Although humans are increasingly in the habit of using deliberation and discursive techniques to reach communal decisions we are unfortunately not that good at it. It takes a long time, compromises are rushed and the result is unsatisfactory. This is another reason why Seeley argued we have much to learn from how honeybees make their decisions. For democracy to exist, deliberation has to be more impressive. Politicians must refine their discursive techniques. So too should civil societies and other governing bodies. We should, like honeybees, be able to reach good decisions in much shorter amounts of time.

Individuals need to be capable of acknowledging the frailties and fallibilities of their own democracies. Australian political philosopher Mark Chou (2011, 2012, 2013) points to how sacred democracy is today. It is near blasphemy to speak of alternatives to democracy. Chou stresses the need for individuals to understand the way their democracies are

DOI: 10.1057/9781137338662

built and what risks their particular system poses to the maintenance of that democracy. In other words, we have to recognize that any good democracy carries with it the seeds of its own destruction. Citizenries can vote a democracy into a monarchy. The division of power can be used to manipulate democratic institutions to create a fake system where citizens think they have a voice but in actuality do not. These are two examples of democide. There are many others. By recognizing these dangers, we become aware of them. Awareness leads to the mitigation of these democidal risks. It offers directions away from political apathy.

The democide angle brings the work of Finnish political theorist Lauri Rapeli into play. He is a mixed-methods thinker who uses empirical studies to establish his points. Rapeli has demonstrated that a majority of citizens are today lacking in even the most basic political and social knowledge. There are not many people that can name each individual that compose the cabinet or executive of their respective governments. Those who can are seldom able to identify which portfolios these politicians hold. It is even harder to keep track of who represents your interests at the local, provincial/state, federal and multinational levels of government. A larger portion of individuals in federal systems are able to identify their direct representatives but the numbers are not exactly promising. What Rapeli's work points to is a fundamental problem with the knowledge that individuals *should* have to be able to better participate in the act of self-government. When reading his works I felt that we should increase non-partisan political education in compulsory schooling and then do something a little crazier: add standardized knowledge-testing as a requisite for voters. If we tie this in with more robust 'vote-compasses'[4] then we should have the makings of a slightly more impressive electoral body.

The final thinker that I would like to include in this overture is the British social theorist David Beetham. He has argued for a remarkable change to happen if we are serious about realizing an actual democracy. His point is that parliament should be separated from political parties. Parliament or congress is a building. Political parties and politicians come and go but the building stays: it is an institution embodied by a physical structure. For Beetham it is about creating space between parliament and the people that do politics under its roof (this includes the senate and the executive for those systems that have them). If there is a separation, what role does this space play? Can other actors be brought into parliament and, if so, what will they do?

For democracy to exist that space in between politicians and parliament should be filled by citizens, bureaucrats and experts. We can attach a body of randomly selected citizens to mirror legislatures and administrations. The role of these individuals will be to participate, communicate and deliberate. A body of bureaucrats, serving parliament and not a government or political party, would act as investigative accountants, journalists, ethics managers and any other useful function. This could result in the greater monitorism of politicians and an increase in their discursive abilities. Finally, universities can bid for a space in parliament to conduct research, consult for politicians and bureaucrats, and, in partnership with the citizens and bureaucrats, propose cutting-edge ideas for legislative consideration.

I too have a role to play with regard to this heuristic of 'democracy on the horizon'. My opinion may change after we achieve a scientific definition of democracy. But for now I maintain that we cannot achieve our democratic aims without establishing the following conditions: that politicians should undergo standardized education just as doctors, plumbers, dentists, electricians, lawyers, carpenters, teachers, and philosophers do. If a citizen is interested in running for election he or she should undergo a 'politician's degree' and swear a Socratic Oath or something in similar vein to the Hippocratic Oath that doctors swear. This would ingrain a common code of ethics against which politicians can be measured by a type of professional review committee: this could help to keep politicians more honest. It would be one more area evaluating the quality of political performance. The educational aspect would help prepare leaders for the act of governing. It would instil a new level of performance expectations. For those who graduate from the degree, but are not elected, they will be in stronger positions to understand what those in office are doing – or should be doing. It could increase monitory democracy.

Politicians holding positions in cabinet (executive) should not at the same time be expected to represent their constituencies. Politicians who are to hold specific portfolios should be directly elected by the citizenry and not by a political party. Is it too much to ask that individuals take notice of who is going to govern one or more of their most valued services? Should the decision of who will be minister or secretary of education or health not come from voters? During general elections it would be a boon to know who is running for which portfolio and how their platforms differentiate. The different dynamics of having individually elected members in the cabinet is interesting to think about. Would

DOI: 10.1057/9781137338662

this destroy the capacity for representative rule in the way we know it today? I think that it would improve the quality of governance as politicians holding portfolios would strive to perform for their public service rather than to tow the party line. That being said, these types of ministers would still suffer from the politicking that occurs between parties in parliament. Making unscrupulous deals and breaking electoral promises are better mitigated through Beetham's proposals. By directly electing portfolio-holding politicians we are also enabling individuals to run for the only purpose of representing their constituencies, not to climb the political ladder and juggle several responsibilities at the same time.

There is also the question of taxation. Citizens are typically not in the strongest position to determine how much they will be taxed. They have little say in how their economies will be run, and, fundamentally, where their tax moneys will be spent. This includes how tax moneys *are* spent. It is common for individuals to pay sales taxes, property taxes, income taxes, airport taxes and various contractual taxes like estate or capital-gains taxes (i.e. when a property transfers from one person to another). It is uncommon for us to know exactly how much tax we have spent in a calendar year – especially in regards to sales taxes. It is equally uncommon for us to know where our tax contributions are being held, who decides where to use them, how they are to be used and what they are in the end buying or paying off. I am uncomfortable with the idea that my tax money might be spent on a poorly performing politician's salary, that it might be used to buy munitions that kill people, that it might be used to subsidize polluting industries, that it might be used to help cater overly expense multinational summits (why not serve a bowl of rice, fufu, or beans to these representatives as the majority of people in the world subsist off these staples?) or that my tax money might be used to pay for the torture of extrajudicial prisoners.

Democracy cannot be achieved unless a capacious and inclusive citizenry can decide on and verify their taxes. My proposition would be for us to develop a system that associates a serialized number to each unit of currency we spend in taxes. We could use a 'tax file number' for identification. For sales taxes, hardware would need to be installed in stores. And a chip would need to be placed inside a type of 'tax card' which we would touch during a transaction. That would associate our number with the sale and the amount of sales tax paid. This money would then be serialized and registered on our tax profile. That would necessitate the development of a software system that holds our 'tax profiles'. We could log-in to this system online to see how much we have been taxed, where the money is held, where it went and who signed off on it. With this kind of profile in place, we could put exclusions on our taxes. In other words, I could decide that my money is to be spent *only* buying equipment for schools, paying a teacher's salary, subsidizing medicine for free medical or dental clinics and paying for the rice that I think should be eaten by our representatives at the G20. Despite its many logistical hurdles and political problems, this system definitively establishes us, the citizenry, as the paymasters of the government. It brings us closer to a number of ideals in contemporary democracies.

We are continuously on the cusp of getting to democracy or being democratic. Many voice whether this will be an interminable process. They ask whether we are going to move from achievement to achievement indefinitely. We ask whether we can ever become a non-violent citizenry, or whether we will reach a point of singularity in the theory and practice of democracy. To be clear, I do not think that my model or its underlying theory will be this singularity. It will, rather, provide a first foundation of democracy. This foundation will need to be built upon. It will be investigated in a multitude of ways to challenge its underlying logic. And we will need to figure out where to go from that first foundation to the next and better one.

The heuristic of 'democracy on the horizon' that I use in this part of Chapter 3 is subjective. Others reading this work might argue that the thinkers I cite do recognize democracy and are not claiming that it will not exist until their views are achieved. In this light, the evidence that I offer argues for *better* democracy to exist, for democracy to *function more effectively*, or for democracy to *survive*. It is a portrayal of an evolutionary story. We try to understand previous or current flawed democracies. We try to make them better. Moral judgements drive this process. We think that democracy will lead to a better place.

There are, however, still those individuals who exclaim 'what democracy is this?' They are the many individuals in apathy, in disillusion and disdain over this forbidden forest that ostensibly brings benefits to the people on its edges. 'Democracy does not exist until we achieve x, y, and z' is no different from 'democracy can be made better if we achieve a, b, and c'. This is because I, and no one else in this world, can possibly know what democracy is. It is a variation on the case of Schrödinger's cat. Democracy has existed and evolved for a long time or it has not. It exists or it does not. It is alive or dead or somewhere in between. The

DOI: 10.1057/9781137338662

only way to know is to open a door. But in our case we first need to build the room that holds the door. We still need to stuff it with post-foundational democracy data (the cat). Every time we run an analysis on this data it is an act of 'closing and opening the door'. I suspect that, at the end, we will find the cat alive with a long and complicated story to tell: democracy was a manifestation of altruism which began in its most basic form during the dawn of life. It came into the complexity we see it in today due to a myriad of factors. Democracy was not founded by the French, English or American Revolutions. Basic democracy has been with humans all along. We have just been enacting it in different ways depending on which spaces, times, agents and constructs we look to.

This point is not meant to disparage achievements that we think are central to this thing called 'democracy'. But we cannot definitively say that they are achievements for democracy until we know what democracy is. As I stated in the Introduction, the work is about recontextualizing democratic things. It is about situating the dominant narratives alongside the subaltern and unknown narratives in the grand planetary picture of democracy across time and space. It is meant to enhance the real victories and dispel the pretenders.

Notes

1 The Girondins were a political faction that felt, in the early 1790s, that the revolution was proceeding too quickly. The Montagnards were also a political faction during that time and were, we think, the drivers of radicalism during the revolution. The Montagnards were associated with the Jacobins. When the Girondins tried to resist the radicalism of the Montagnards, they were met with furious and murderous violence. Historians argue that this is one possible starting point for the period many today know as the Reign of Terror.
2 A battle in 480 BCE between an alliance of Greek states and the Persian Empire happened around these Straits. This battle is regarded as a turning point for the history of democracy as this victory demonstrated the strength of democratic Hellas over despotic Persia.
3 Keane (2009) uses the term 'pluriverse' to make this point.
4 A vote-compass is a tool designed to increase 'electoral literacy'. It helps people who do not know much about politics to identify where they are situated in relation to every political party's platform. It aids individuals to cast better votes for whatever election a vote-compass is being used in.

DOI: 10.1057/9781137338662

4
Schrödinger's Democracy

Abstract: *In this final chapter we zoom out from the material introduced in Chapters 1 to 3. The argument that basic democracy is not a human invention is first offered. We then move to answer a number of questions raised throughout the book: 'where did democracy come from?', 'how did its complexity arise?' and 'what, in the end, is democratic?' These are our main questions. It is a look to the future. It is a critical consideration of what the theory of evolutionary basic democracy and its model can bring to politics and society.*

Gagnon, Jean-Paul. *Evolutionary Basic Democracy: A Critical Overture*, Basingstoke: Palgrave Macmillan, 2013. DOI: 10.1057/9781137338662.

Austrian physicist Erwin Schrödinger proposed a thought experiment in 1935. It was about a cat in a sealed room. Inside the room are a Geiger counter and a piece of radioactive element. The element is thought to decay a little every hour. If the Geiger counter registers this decay it releases a switch. That switch sprays poisonous gas into the room. This kills the cat. But because the room is sealed, and there are no cameras or windows, the scientist cannot tell whether the cat is alive or dead. The only way of finding this out is for the scientist to open the door. The act of opening the door interferes with the experiment: it entangles[1] the scientist in the result. In other words, we affect the result of studies by participating in them and by interpreting their results. If the scientist does not open the door the cat is both alive and dead at the same time. It is a paradox. And studies, as far as we know, are useless to us unless we can explain their results. We have to become entangled.

I see a similar situation with democracy. As mentioned at the end of Chapter 3, democracy needs scientists to engage it. We need to build a room (planetary time and space model) that can have a cat in it (planetary democracy data). We can forego the poison and Geiger death trap. We need to run as many experiments on this data as possible. Every time an experiment is launched, a particular door is sealed, and we cannot see the cat for a time. But when the experiment is finished and we open to door to check our result, we become entangled with it. If we can measure *how* each user became entangled with the experiment and how the experiment was affected by each user we could come closer to the findings we need. Because each study is subjective, understanding the nature of entanglement would help to identify the tenuous foundations of the results coming from this mass of studies. It would help us create a first scientific post-foundation of democracy, one to be built upon again and again until something akin to a singularity of democracy is reached. This is an ultimate telos for this book.

Politics and society can change by reaching a widely agreed upon scientific foundation for democracy. This change would be the result of knowing, with the best confidence we humans can have, what is democracy and what is not. This, over time, with new and better scientific foundations would lead to a mastery of certain things. It would lead to an evolution of the human–animal. Non-violence, equality, effective topics for communication, easily selecting better leaders and creating impressively informed communal long-term goals could be the unshakeable foundations of a future human existence. Competition between individuals and associations over new ways to drive humanity forward would be fierce. But it would be a morally grounded competitive ferocity supported by cooperation, like an extremely competitive sporting match between the most ethical athletes imaginable. This kind of competition would foster the growth and strengthening of social fabrics. Not burning these fabrics to ash which we are currently, and unfortunately, in the habit of doing. But this is a discussion on futurism in democratic theory. It is but another best guess.

In this closing chapter I discuss certain unresolved arguments in the literature covered in preceding parts of the book. The aim is to identify and then discuss the problems that need resolving for the theory of evolutionary basic democracy (EBD) to proceed. Three main questions are asked: where does democracy come from, how did its complexity emerge, and, in the end, what is democracy and what is not. The answers to these questions in this book come from the old ontology. Any works of this sort cannot escape that fact. For the answers to those questions to be reproducible, non-parochial and positivist, they would have to use the complete data from the model presented in the Introduction. As that analytical tool is now only being built, I must try to offer answers through other means. But before proceeding in that direction, there are minor questions that need fuller engagements.

Why are nonhumans incapable of having democracy or being democratic? This question does not have a recognizable debate in the literature. It does, however, relate to Isakhan's and Stockwell's work that questions why 'primitive' is associated with democracy when we speak of it in archaic times. The same question can be asked about quasi, proto and semi prefixes to democracy. Why use these things? Isakhan's question 'what's so primitive about democracy?' is poignant. Individual human beings 10,000 years ago held assemblies. They used verbal communication. And they had deliberations that were needed to make collective decisions just as we do today. Ancient democracy in the Teutoberg forest, on the Nile Delta, in the Indo–Gangetic plain and on the Siberian tundra is probably not different to how smaller numbers of individuals do democracy today. Given the limited amount of knowledge that we have about archaic democracies it does not seem fair to use denigrating qualifiers when describing them. This point extends to the way hunter–gatherer societies today govern themselves. What, in the end, is so primitive about their egalitarian assemblies and deliberations?

DOI: 10.1057/9781137338662

But that point and the questions it raises remain anthropocentric. Although further research is required it seems that Homo sapiens were capable of inter-breeding with at least Neanderthals and Denisovans.[2] We are probably composed of other hominoid genetics from breeding that occurred over millions of years. After all, we share genes with slime-moulds, primates and mole-rats. Those had to come from somewhere. This point is essential to link us as one type of animal out of numerous others that can behave democratically. Although it is difficult to prove that Neanderthals or Homo erectus held egalitarian assemblies, made collective decisions and had ways of rotating leadership, it is likely that some of them did. This is true for times of resource abundance where the stress of survival does not blow out the delicate flames of democratic behaviours. This reasoning comes from the argument that cooperation and friendly competition among relatively equal agents seems to make for the best survival chances. Democratic behaviours are phenomena observed in wild animals, certain of which significantly predate Homo sapiens as a species. The manifestation of altruism through democratic behaviours from the dawn of life is a controversial point, but one that I think deserves championing until proven otherwise.

The separation between human democracy and nonhuman democracy is made clearest by the arguments in Chapter 3. Democracy is a social and political phenomenon. It is moral: for democracy to exist it must meet certain basic moral and practical functions. For the moral side today, democracy means equality for everyone – the same chances, the same support and the same power so that individuals can compete on the same playing field. Gender disappears – we are all human individuals. In a democracy there cannot be corruption, a lack of accountability and poor transparency. The government and governance must manifest itself from the collective of individuals. *L'etat c'est moi* holds true for each person. You do not live in a country. The country lives because of you.

The statements in the paragraph above synthesize the arguments we looked at in Chapter 3. For democracy to exist, moral expectations have to be realized through institutions. Individuals have to see that impressive efforts are at work to increase and maintain the 'good society'. The emphasis here is that a working democracy requires high cognition, complex institutions and moral post-foundations. Democracy is hard for humans to achieve. Because it is so difficult, how can nonhumans expect to be democratic or to have their own democracies?

DOI: 10.1057/9781137338662

One answer is in scale. Like humans, nonhumans are continuously evolving. Bees, ants, whales, metazoans and yeast evolved as they are today the same way humans did: through trial and error. What worked best propagated species. And for the bacteria to massive cetaceans that we looked at in this book it seems that basic democracy (cooperation and positive competition among relative equals) was a best method for survival. As individual nonhumans scale into larger numbers the type of basic democratic practice changes. Bats, fish, insects and microbes have a burden of communication the greater their numbers become. In these higher population settings hierarchical systems are sometimes more effective than egalitarian ones. But do human democracies not build delicate hierarchies that are meant to shift and change like the sands of a desert? The honeybee uses more experienced (older) bees and quorum formation to make surprisingly accurate decisions which the majority of other bees 'trust'. This is why I term the honeybee system an elite, or expert, democracy. We as humans may not agree with the hierarchical honeybee system but it works for them.

Another answer is in chance. Why do bees do democratic things one way and ants another? Why do humans have so many competing variations of democracy across time and space? As time advanced and species experienced different challenges they made adjustments. Basic democracy grew into a specific manifestation. For microbes this explanation is especially apparent. A group of bacteria communicates with chemical signals. The group encounters an antibiotic. Bacteria detect the death of other bacteria. Few individuals survive the antibiotic. One undergoes mitosis or shares its genetics with other individuals. The group eventually becomes resistant to the antibiotic. Without communication and cooperation the microbe would not be able to face this adversity. This is one reason why antibiotic resistance in bacteria is a serious medical issue. In the end, basic democracy is present in animate matter. It manifests differently depending on what species we look at, when in time and where in space. This holds true for humans too.

That particular viewpoint is what drove the development of the model I presented in the Introduction. If basic democracy is theorized as a constant for humans and nonhumans then it probably is manifested in various ways outside of the 'west'. It formed a long time ago as certain creatures figured out that an equal playing field, cooperation, communication, frequent changes in leadership and being able to differentiate one group from another held survival benefits. Basic democracy has

DOI: 10.1057/9781137338662

led to various manifestations of democratic phenomena anywhere we look. Some will be extremely simple and will do only one democratic thing well. Others will do a number of things well but may not be considered democracies because certain core parameters, like collective decision-making, are suppressed. Some are in serious tension with anti-democratic elements. Others seem poised to continue with their systems, dabbling here and evolving there. But just as anyone else who has proposed a theory of democracy – I could be wrong. It is important to stress that the most important part of this book is the model that we have been reverse engineering over the past few chapters. That is where the right answers will come from and where current best guesses will be proven or disproven.

With that established it would be good to return to our main line of questioning. How is democracy solely bound to Homo sapiens? The arguments described in Chapter 3 share the premise that democracy is a human affair. I built the heuristic where a number of scholars argue that democratic humanity has still not reached this zenith. But how is this anthropocentricism possible given the arguments presented in Chapters 1 and 2? One answer is that humans do not have a foundation of democracy which can be used to compare existing systems. Is *x* democratic according to our post-foundationally established and globally agreed upon positivist *y*? The other is that nonhumans have not yet evolved the ability to fundamentally alter the rules of their system as quickly as humans do. This may be why the democratic behaviour of species seems to remain consistent unless disrupted by changes to their environment. Humans evolved through democratic practice in resistance to anti-democratic elements. We seem, however, to have lost track of what it was, what it now is and where it should be going. Democracy in its most basic form cannot be considered a solely human creation.

Where does democracy come from?

This question is useful to begin with as we have been addressing it for the majority of this book. Chapters 1 and 2 describe a body of literature that supports the argument of basic democracy emerging in the beginnings of time and space. This was tracked through an argument that began by looking at strange concepts: 'prebiotic democracy', 'the democracy of sperm', 'microbial democracy', and 'animal democracy'.

DOI: 10.1057/9781137338662

In the Introduction I also mentioned 'dendrite democracy' (democracy between synapses in the brain). Democracy in this context is a mixture of cooperation and friendly competition. This type of competition is one that sees the outcome of the contest as a boon for the greater good. The unfriendly type of competition, where the outcome is a boon for an individual at the expense of the rest, is often punished. In nature, if an individual forsakes the group this sometimes manifests in their death. Cooperation does not replace but rather joins the cut-throat type of competition which has been argued as the universal rule of evolution.

Democracy does not start in the fabric of matter itself. Yes, particles of dust, prebiotics, amino acids, sugar molecules, oxygen atoms and numerous other building blocks of life do things together. But this way of working together to build more complex chains is driven by amoral physical forces. There is no decision to make: it just happens that certain prebiotics bind with others to randomly produce things under the right conditions. As seen in Chapter 2, why anything from electrons to the tons of matter involved in the formation of stars come together and make different things is still a place of uncertainty. The mainstream position has it that natural laws dictate that should a, b and c be found together in the presence of x, y and z they are *forced* to obey. Natural laws dictate that continuously evolving inanimate and animate matter occurs through chance. Atoms sometimes *share* electrons; molecules somehow have receptors to *bind* with others; and new matter can emerge through the *inclusion* of certain gases, liquids, solids and energies in a vacuum. But these are our representations and only reveal the subjectivity of the user. It does not reveal the intentions of inanimate matter. That kind of matter does not have intentions.

In Chapter 3 we looked specifically at the moral arguments of democracy. This is the narrative that I present as being in disagreement with the evolutionary perspective. For some, democracy began in Greece. For others it began in the USA and for others still it has yet to come. These arguments differ because they say that a suite of different institutions, capacities and behaviours are required for a democracy to exist or to better exist. In this context democracy comes from many places. Even though democracy began somewhere it is not as good as it could be. This reinforces the perspective that better democracy, more democracy or democracy itself, will emerge in the future. Most argue that we are working on this stuff now. Some argue that democracy is a never ending process.

> Democracy is a theory, policy, procedure, and art, emphasizing human welfare, individual freedom, popular participation and general tolerance. It can adapt itself to many conditions, but it thrives in an atmosphere of education, toleration, peace and prosperity. Ignorance, dogma, war and poverty are its enemies. They breed absolute and arbitrary government, uncritical and lethargic to people, which are the reverse of democracy. (Quincy Wright in Paris, 10 March 1949)

The contestations and continuations of democracy argued on moral grounds are important. But so too is building different foundational stages of democracy itself. This will increase the quality of the different moralistic interpretations of basic democracy and lead not to a utopia or dystopia, but a better way of governing and structuring government until an even better way eventually emerges. Different types of polity should practice democracy in a way that best suits their structures and agents. A small town for example would benefit from a different interpretation of basic democracy than the type followed by a federated state. The landscape remains the same but the practices of the peoples on that land and their buildings should be different.

Democracy in the context of Chapter 3 is not a natural property. It is the conscious decision of educated individuals who decide to create it in order to protect a teleology of what the good society is. That being said, democracy in the context of Chapters 1 and 2 is a natural property. Particles, microbes and animals do democracy to different extents. Some nonhumans certainly have perfected particular democratic traits. For prebiotics it seems that cooperation is compulsory. But for honeybees, as far as we know, individuals seem to make carefully decided and conscious choices. Democracy is more complicated than we have long presumed.

How did more than 50 types of democracy emerge?

The position on origins in Chapter 3 helps to describe why numerous democracy theories, concepts, practices and their nuances emerged. In one sense it is due to a lack of a foundation capable of describing democracy for all of planetary time and space, not just Homo sapiens' time and space. This missing foundation leads individuals to argue for different foundations and to try to justify those points with impressive evidence and logic. In another sense, even if a planetary foundation were achieved

DOI: 10.1057/9781137338662

in a manner agreeable to the majority of experts, this would still spawn a complexity as the foundation itself would be interpreted differently. Indeed, the foundation would be used to engineer democratic systems that would best fit the polity in question. From that perspective it is possible to understand that different foundations each establish their own different interpretations which lead to more variety and contestation. A scientific foundation for democracy will improve the quality of these manifestations. It will sort what is democratic from what is not.

That is my explanation for why democracy is enormously complex today. As time went by and individuals came into contact with the political, social and economic arguments of democracy, the literature grew, and its diversity became greater. This, and a lack of a morally viable alternative, helped to drive interest in the subject. Below I present as an example a list of democracies. Even though it is a large list, and I have provided arbitrary sub-lists for certain cases (most cases would have one or more sub-lists), it is still the surface of a more complicated body. For reasons of space, the focus in the list provided is anthropocentric. I have not included nonhuman democracies.

A number of the categories in the listed in Table 4.1 can mean the same thing. 'American' democracy today can mean a 'presidential', 'constitutional', 'liberal', 'deliberative', 'associational' and 'hollow' democracy depending on how a person understands it. 'American' democracy would also mean different things if we looked at different time periods. The main function that the list in Table 4.1 has is to demonstrate the type of complexity we currently face with regard to democracy. How do we make sense of these things if we do not know what democracy is?

TABLE 4.1 *A list of different democracies*

1. Liberal
   a. Neoliberal
2. Conservative
   a. Neoconservative
3. Social
4. Aristocratic
   a. Tsarist Russia
   b. Baronial Poland
   c. Monarchic Spain
5. Republican
   a. Neo-republican
6. Christian
   a. Catholic
   b. Protestant
   c. Anglican
7. Islamic
   a. Shia
   b. Sunni
8. Buddhist
9. Baha'i
10. Confucian
    a. Neo-Confucian
11. Bourgeois
12. Workers'

Continued

DOI: 10.1057/9781137338662

TABLE 4.1 *Continued*

- a. Proletarian
13. Representative
14. Direct
15. Deliberative
    - a. Conventional
    - b. Cooperative
    - c. Collaborative
16. Radical
17. Agonistic
    - a. Oppositional
    - b. Expressive
    - c. Constitutional
    - d. Adversarial
    - e. Responsive
    - f. Liberal
18. Environmental
    - a. Ecological
    - b. Green
    - c. Sustainable
19. Electronic
20. Primitive
21. Electoral
22. Participatory
23. Consociational
24. Discursive
25. Monitory
26. Presidential
27. Parliamentary
28. Legal
29. Federal
30. Nation-State
31. Multinational
32. Provincial
33. Municipal
34. Global
35. Basic
36. Evolutionary
37. Universal
38. Ecumenical
39. Cosmopolitan
40. Regional
41. Communist
42. Anarchist
43. Consensus
44. Iroquois
45. Sami
46. Inuit
47. Highland Papua New Guinean
48. Aboriginal (there could be hundreds here)
49. Native American (possibly hundreds here as well especially if we include indigenous nations from the Latin American Region)
50. Interactive
51. Associational
52. American
53. Nordic
54. Russian
55. Chinese
56. Greek
57. French
58. Sortal
    - a. Quasi
    - b. Semi
    - c. Partial
59. Scalar
    - a. Low
    - b. Medium
    - c. High/Full
60. Imperial
61. De-militarized
    - a. Cost Rica
    - b. Kiribati
    - c. Liechtenstein
    - d. Saint Vincent and the Grenadines
    - e. Saint Lucia
    - f. Palau
62. False
    - a. Ersatz
    - b. Fake
    - c. Phoney
    - d. Bogus
    - e. Insubstantial
    - f. Hollow

As I argued in the Introduction, I think we need to work collaboratively to populate the model of evolutionary basic democracy (EBD). With the complexity of democracy increasingly defined we can then deploy reproducible studies. With these we can unleash the power of computational analyses. Over time we can conduct meta-analyses of the results of studies that each asks 'what are your shared characteristics?' We can then use Schrödinger's focus on entanglement to determine the subjectivity of all these different experiments. The median of the studies' results and the median of the users' subjectivity would give us a good starting foundation to work from.

To date the standard practice of making sense of different types of democracy, termed modelism, is to choose certain parameters that we think are central to democracy and then to measure the world for them. That approach to categorizing democracy's complexity is being resisted by post-foundationalists.

All of the items from the list above have 'democracy', 'democratic', or 'democratization' literature associated with them. A number of them like 'deliberative', 'representative', 'liberal' and 'social' have vast literatures. A standard library catalogue search excluding newspaper articles, book reviews and trade publications reveals 7,902 hits for 'deliberative democracy', 17, 553 hits for 'representative democracy' and 36, 841 hits for 'liberal democracy'. It would be difficult to sort one of these bodies out let alone have total command of it. As mentioned in the Introduction, their size makes it improbable for one individual to understand or even know of them all. That was a primary reason for the development of EBD as a theory and the creation of its working model. We have a pressing need to both describe and make sense of these grand complexities. The model is an analytic tool for organizational and descriptive programs. But it is not in its current state highly effective at presenting different types of democracy. We need a different tool to achieve that.

One useful method would be to borrow the periodic table framework from the sciences. The periodic table presents known chemical elements. It organizes 118 elements in several ways: by atomic number, blocks, periods and groups. Solids, liquids, gases and elements with no definitive state are separated in ways that describe trends in their behaviour. The table is useful for scientists in numerous fields. It helps to drive their research.

In the study of democracy we do not have a similar framework. There certainly are efforts by scholars to collect, identify and describe, for example, various participatory institutions (e.g. Participedia); institutions for accountability, transparency and anti-corruption (e.g. the United Nations Convention against Corruption); and institutions for the improvement of parliamentary practices (e.g. the Inter-Parliamentary Union). But these are not looking to present the theories, concepts and practices of democracy as a whole. We lack the big picture.

We can, for example, organize the different types of democracy we have on two simple axes: time and number of individuals. This would see the numerically few, small, groups of individuals from 500,000 years ago contrast with the tens of thousands of citizens in ancient Athens 2,500 years ago. We could group democracies by type of assembly, type of representation, type of monitorism, type of participation and type of citizenry. Small local assemblies would contrast with large federal parliaments. Presidential systems would contrast with Ministerial systems. Such a table of contents for the entire planet would be large and would require consolidation. Historical assemblies such as Swiss Cantons, German folkmoots, New England town hall meetings and Iroquoian village meetings could be grouped into the 'small assembly' category. Contemporary France, Germany, Canada, Australia and South Africa could, for example, be grouped under 'representative systems'. The key would be for us to know when to group the same governing methods and to separate those with differences.

A 'democracy table' of this sort is essential for us to organize theories, concepts and practices of democracy. The model given in the Introduction is a vacuum cleaner. Its purpose is to suck up all of the democracy data available to us across all languages. It then organizes these data across time and space. This allows us to quickly identify knowledge gaps and to deploy reproducible studies on this unprecedented democracy dataset. But it does not categorize in the way a periodic table can. A 'democracy table' then would be valuable to have.

What is democratic and what is not?

This, at the end, is the question that begs to be answered. Under the current conditions where parts of the complexity of democracy are ill-defined and its full complexity unknown, it is not possible to say in a scientific and positivist way what democracy is or is not. It is the subjective, moral decisions that individuals make today which argue matters to be democratic or not. Some are more democratic than others. Some democracies are not welcomed by other democracies. Some governments claim to have democracy and others are accused of not

DOI: 10.1057/9781137338662

being democratic. Somewhere in that mixture we have the ability to try to achieve what we think of as democracy. Until we reach a positivist conception of basic democracy we will continue to be bound by the current politics of the discourse. North Korea will, for example, continue to claim it is democratic because there is no way to *prove* its rulers wrong. We can certainly argue that the regime is wrong and use hard or soft power mechanisms to force or encourage its rulers into obeisance of the international community. But we will not at the end be certain of what we are advocating by the emphasis of 'democratization' and the demonstration of 'real existing democracies'.

Humans have difficulties determining the democracy of their own species. I maintain that the arguments stating democracy to be a solely human invention are invalid. Indeed, foundational claims on any theory of democracy as being 'the' democracy for the planet are also invalid. We would do well to recall that these claims can only logically argue the foundations of specific types of democracy: not democracy itself. This is because we do not yet have the methods for so doing. I hope that this book can help in that regard. It is important to note that EBD does not make the claim to founding a conception of planetary democracy. It is designed, rather, to argue that we lack this foundation. It then proposes a way for reaching it. We are left then with the task of working collaboratively toward the fulfilment of a positivist foundation. It appears to be the best way forward.

Notes

1 I use the English meaning of 'entanglement' here and not the technical term used by physicists. I owe a specific debt to Dr Alex Stilgoe and Dr Timo Nieminen for helping me to understand the technical meaning.

2 Denisova hominin were, in March 2010, announced as a human species that existed approximately 40,000 years ago.

DOI: 10.1057/9781137338662

Works Cited

Abdalla, Mohamad and Halim Rane. 2011. 'Behind a Veil: Islam's Democratic History'. In Benjamin Isakhan and Stephen Stockwell's *The Secret History of Democracy*. Basingstoke, UK: Palgrave Macmillan, pp. 79–91.

Adami, Christoph, Charles Ofria and Travis C. Collier. 2000. 'Evolution of Biological Complexity'. *PNAS*, 97 (9): 4463–4468.

Adler, Julius and Wung-Wai Tso. 1974. '"Decision"-Making in Bacteria: Chemotactic Response of Escherichia coli Conflicting Stimuli'. *Science*, 184 (4143): 1292–1294.

Agamben, Giorgio. 1998. *Homo Sacer: Sovereign Power and Bare Life*. Stanford: Stanford University Press.

Al-Jabri, Mohammed Abed. 2008. *Democracy, Human Rights and Law in Islamic Thought*. London: I. B. Tauris.

Alonso, Sonia, John Keane and Wolfgang Merkel. 2011. *The Future of Representative Democracy*. Cambridge, UK: Cambridge University Press.

Ambridge, Lindsay June. 2007. 'Searching History: The Non-Elite in Ancient Egypt'. *History Compass*, 5 (2): 632–645.

Arblaster, Anthony. 2002. *Democracy*. 3rd edn. Buckingham, UK: Open University Press.

Arendt, Hannah. 2007. 'The Great Tradition II. Ruling and Being Ruled'. *Social Research*, 74 (4): 941–954.

Arjomand, Saïd Amir. 2004. 'Coffeehouses, Guilds and Oriental Despotism Government and Civil Society in Late 17th to Early 18th Century Istanbul and Isfahan, and as Seen from Paris and London'. *European Journal of Sociology*, 45 (1): 23–42.

DOI: 10.1057/9781137338662

Asmonti, Luca. 2006. 'The Arginusae Trial, the Changing Role of Strategoi and the Relationship Between Demos and Military Leadership in Late Fifth-Century Athens'. *Bulletin – Institute of Classical Studies*, 49 (1): 1–21.

Barley, Stephen R. 2007. 'Corporations, Democracy and the Public Good'. *Journal of Management Inquiry*, 16 (3): 201–215.

Barnwell, Paul S. and Marco Mostert. 2003. *Political Assemblies in the Earlier Middle Ages*. Belgium: Turnhout Brepols Publishers.

Benedict, Catherine, Matt Geisler, Johan Trygg, Norman Huner and Vaughan Hurry. 2006. 'Consensus by Democracy: Using Meta-Analyses of Microarray and Genomic Data to Model to Cold Acclimation Signalling Pathway in Arabidopsis'. *Plant Physiology*, 141 (4): 1219–1232.

Bennett, N. and C. Faulkes. 2000. *African Mole-rats: Ecology and Eusociality*. Cambridge, UK: Cambridge University Press.

Ben-Jacob, E. 2008. 'Social Behavior of Bacteria: from Physics to Complex Organisation'. *The European Physical Journal B*, 65: 315–322.

Bertrand, Claude-Jean (ed.) 2003. *An Arsenal for Democracy: Media Accountability Systems*. Creskill, NJ: Hampton Press.

Birch, Sarah. 2011. *Electoral Malpractice*. Oxford, UK: Oxford University Press.

Black, Antony. 2009. *A World History of Ancient Political Thought*. Oxford, UK: Oxford University Press.

Black, J. 1988. 'Preflight Signalling in Swans – A Mechanism for Group Cohesion and Flock Formation'. *Ethology*, 79: 143–157.

Boehm, Christopher. 2012. 'Prehistory'. In Benjamin Isakhan and Stephen Stockwell *The Edinburgh Companion to the History of Democracy*. Edinburgh, UK: Edinburgh University Press. Pages 29–39.

Böhmer, Martin, Qui Van, Ingo Weyand, Volker Hagen, Michael Bayermann, Midori Matsumoto, Motonori Hoshi, Eilo Hildebrand and Ulrich Benjamin Kaupp. 2005. 'Ca^2+ Spikes in the Flagellum Control Chemotactic Behavior of Sperm'. *The Embo Journal*, 24 (15): 2741–2752.

Bonner, J. T. and D. S. Lamont. 2005. 'Behaviour of Cellular Slime Moulds in the Soil'. *Mycologia*, 97 (1): 178–184.

Boomsma, Jacobus J. 2011. 'Evolutionary Biology: Farming Writ Small'. *Nature*, 469: 308–309.

Boulhosa, Patricia Pires. 2011. 'Ideals and Aspirations: Democracy and Law-Making in Medieval Iceland'. In Benjamin Isakhan and Stephen

Stockwell *The Secret History of Democracy.* Basingstoke, UK: Palgrave Macmillan, pp. 92–104.
Bourke, Richard. 2008. 'Enlightenment, Revolution and Democracy'. *Constellations,* 15 (1): 10–32.
Bozzone, Donna M. 1997. 'Feeding Behaviors in Cellular Slime Moulds: A Microbial System to Study Competition'. *The American Biology Teacher,* 59 (9): 565–572.
Brännäs, Eva, Anders Alanärä and Carin Magnhagen. 2001. 'The Social Behaviour of Fish'. In Linda J. Keeling and Harold W. Gonyou *Social Behaviour in Farm Animals.* International: CABI.
Brather, Sebastian. 2011. 'The Western Slavs of the Seventh to the Eleventh Century – An Archaeological Perspective'. *History Compass,* 9 (6): 454–473.
Brown, Sam P. and Angus Buckling. 2008. 'A Social Life for Discerning Microbes'. *Cell,* 135 (4): 600–603.
Bukhari, Huzaima and Ikramul Haq. 2010. 'Accountability and Democracy'. *Economic Review,* 41 (2): 50–51.
Burke, Edmund. Edited by Daniel E. Ritchie. 1992 [1790]. *Further Reflections on the French Revolution.* Indianapolis, IN: Liberty Fund.
Campbell, Heather M. 2011. *Advances in Democracy: From the French Revolution to the Present-Day European Union.* London: Britannica Educational Publishing.
Canny, Brian Gerard. 2010. 'The Economics and Ethics of Celtic Ireland'. *Procesos de Mercado* [Market Processes], 7 (2): 215–238.
Cartledge, Paul. 2007. 'Democracy, Origins Of: Contributions to a Debate'. In Kurt A. Raflaub, Josiah Ober and Robert Wallace. *Origins of Democracy in Ancient Greece.* Los Angeles, CA: University of California Press.
Chou, Mark. 2011. 'When Democracies Fail'. *Political Studies Review,* 9 (3): 344–356.
Chou, Mark. 2012. *Greek Tragedy and Contemporary Democracy.* New York: Bloomsbury.
Chou, Mark. 2013. *Theorising Democide: Why and How Democracies Fail.* Basingstoke, UK: Palgrave Macmillan.
Cohen, Elliot D (ed). 2005. *News Incorporated: Corporate Media Ownership and Its Threat to Democracy.* Amherst, NY: Prometheus Books.
Coles, Romand. 2011. 'The Neuropolitical *habitus* of Resonant Receptive Democracy'. *Ethics & Global Politics,* 4 (4): 273–293.

Condorcet, Nicolas de. 1795 [English edition from 1796]. *Outlines of an Historical View of the Progress of the Human Mind.* Philadelphia, USA.

Congleton, Roger. 2011. *Perfecting Parliament: Constitutional Reform and the Origins of Western Democracy.* Cambridge, UK: Cambridge University Press.

Connolly, William E. 1983. 'Discipline, Politics, and Ambiguity'. *Political Theory,* 11 (3): 325–341.

Conrad, L. and T. J. Roper. 2007. 'Democracy in Animals: the Evolution of Shared Group Decisions'. *Proceedings of the Royal Society B – Biological Sciences,* 274 (1623): 2317–2326.

Cornell, Heather N., John M. Marzluff and Shannon Pecoraro. 2011. 'Social Learning Spreads Knowledge about Dangerous Humans Among American Crows'. *Proceedings of the Royal Society B: Biological Sciences,* 279 (1728): 499–508.

Crick, Bernard. 2002. *Democracy: A Very Short Introduction.* Oxford, UK: Oxford University Press.

Curato, Nicole. 2012. 'Respondents as Interlocutors: Translating Deliberative Democratic Principles to Qualitative Interviewing Ethics'. *Qualitative Inquiry,* 18 (7): 571–582.

Dandamayev, M. A. 1995. 'Babylonian Popular Assemblies in the First Millennium BC'. *The Bulletin of the Canadian Society for Mesopotamian Studies,* 30: 23–29.

Davis, Karen M. and Gordon M. Burghardt. 2011. 'Turtles (Pseudemys nelsoni) Learn about Visual Cues Indicating Food from Experienced Turtles'. *Journal of Comparative Psychology,* 125 (4): 404–410.

Della Porta, Donatella and Yves Mény (eds) 1997. *Democracy and Corruption in Europe.* London: Pinter.

Dirmoser, Dietmar. 2005. 'Democracia sin demócratas: Sobre la crisis de la democracia en América Latina'. *Nueva Sociedad,* 197: 28–40.

Dobson, Andrew. 2010. 'Democracy and Nature: Speaking and Listening'. *Political Studies,* 58 (4): 752–768.

Dryzek, John and Jean-Paul Gagnon. 2013. 'Twists of Democratic Governance'. In Jean-Paul Gagnon *Democratic Theorists in Conversation: Turns in Contemporary Thought.* Basingstoke, UK: Palgrave Macmillan.

Dryzek, John and Simon Niemeyer. 2008. 'Discursive Representation'. *American Political Science Review,* 102 (4): 481–493.

Dunn, John. 2005. *Setting the People Free: The Story of Democracy.* London: Atlantic Books.

DOI: 10.1057/9781137338662

Dunn, John and Jean-Paul Gagnon. 2013. 'The Impossibility of "Knowing" Democracy'. In Jean-Paul Gagnon *Democratic Theorists in Conversation: Turns in Contemporary Thought.* Basingstoke, UK: Palgrave Macmillan.
Eckersley, Robyn. 2011. 'Representing Nature'. In Sonia Alonso, John Keane and Wolfgang Merkel's *The Future of Representative Democracy.* Cambridge, UK: Cambridge University Press.
Eckerlsey, Robyn and Jean-Paul Gagnon. 2013. 'Representing Nature and Contemporary Democracy'. *Journal of Democratic Theory* [forthcoming].
Edge, Peter W. and C. C. Augur Pearce. 2006. 'The Development of the Lord Bishop's Role in the Manx Tynwald'. *The Journal of Ecclesiastical History,* 57 (3): 494–514.
Ehrenberg, Victor. 1950. 'Origins of Democracy'. *Historia: Zeitschrift für Alte Geschichte, [Historia: Journal for Ancient History]* 1 (4): 515–548.
Elstub, Stephen. 2010. 'Linking Micro Deliberative Democracy and Decision-Making: Trade-Offs between Theory and Practice in a Partisan Citizen Forum'. *Representation,* 46 (3): 309–324.
Elstub, Stephen and Jean-Paul Gagnon. 2012. 'From Modelism to Ecumenical Democracy through Practical Equilibrium: Deliberative Democracy as Example'. *Journal of Democratic Theory* [forthcoming].
Estlund, David (ed). 2002. *Democracy.* Malden, MA: Blackwell Publishers.
Federle, Michael J. and Bonnie L. Bassler. 2003. 'Interspecies Communication in Bacteria'. *The Journal of Clinical Investigation,* 112 (9): 1291–1299.
Fisher, Heidi S. and Hopi E. Hoekstra. 2010. 'Competition Drives Cooperation Among Closely Related Sperm of Deer Mice'. *Nature,* 463: 801–803.
Fleck, Robert K. and F. Andrew Hanssen. 2006. 'The Origins of Democracy: A Model with Application to Ancient Greece'. *Journal of Law and Economics,* 49 (1): 115–146.
Follett, Mary Parker. 1965 [c1920s]. *The New State: Group Organization, the Solution of Popular Government.* Gloucester, MA: P. Smith.
Foucault, Michel. 1978. *The History of Sexuality, Vol 1: An Introduction.* New York: Pantheon Books.
Frank, Andre Gunder. 1999. 'A Testimonial Contribution to the 25th Anniversary Issue of *Social Justice*'. *Social Justice,* 26 (2): 51–55.
Frommen, Joachim G. and Theo C. M. Bakker. 2004. 'Adult Three-Spined Sticklebacks Prefer to Shoal with Familiar Kin'. *Behaviour,* 141 (11/12): 1401–1409.

Fukuyama, Francis. 2010. 'The "End of History" 20 Years Later'. *New Perspectives Quarterly*, 27 (1): 7–10.
Fukuyama, Francis. 2011. *The Origins of Political Order.* Volume 1. New York: Farrar, Strauss and Giroux.
Fukuyama, Francis. 2012. 'The Future of History'. *Foreign Affairs*, 91 (1): 53–61.
Furuichi, Takeshi. 2011. 'Female Contributions to the Peaceful Nature of Bonobo Society'. *Evolutionary Anthropology: Issues, News and Reviews.* 20 (4): 131–142.
Gagnon, Jean-Paul. 2010. 'Democratic Theory and Theoretical Physics'. *Taiwan Journal of Democracy*, 6 (2): 1–22.
Gagnon, Jean-Paul. 2012. 'An Intervention on "Democracy" as a Term in Empirical Political Analysis'. *Public Administration and Policy: An Asia-Pacific Journal*, 15 (2): 71–96.
Gagnon, Jean-Paul. 2012a. 'Environmental Democracy'. *Political Reflection Magazine*, 3 (4): 6–84.
Gagnon, Jean-Paul. 2012b. 'If Our Underwhelming Politicians Don't Pass the Test, Perhaps It's Time to Make Them Sit One'. *The Conversation*, 16 February. Online source: https://theconversation.edu.au/if-our-underwhelming-politicians-dont-pass-the-test-perhaps-its-time-to-make-them-sit-one-4599. Last accessed: 19/12/2012.
Gallie, W. B. 1956. 'Essentially Contested Concepts'. *Meeting of the Aristotelian Society* at 21 Bedford Square, London, W.C.1, on 12 March, at 7:30 pm.
Gidon, Albert and Idan Segev. 2009. 'Spike-Timing-Dependent Synaptic Plasticity and Synaptic Democracy in Dendrites'. *Journal of Neural Physiology*, 101 (6): 3226–3234.
Gill, Graeme. 2008. *Bourgeoisie, State and Democracy: Russia, Britain, France, Germany, and the USA*. Oxford, UK: Oxford University Press.
Gillin, John Lewis. 1919. 'The Origin of Democracy'. *American Journal of Sociology*, 24 (6): 704–714.
Haba, N., Y. Matsui, N. Okamura and T. Suzuki. 2000. 'Are Lepton Flavor Mixings in the Democratic Mass Matrix Stable against Quantum Corrections?' *Physics Letter B*, 489 (1–2): 184–193.
Hamington, Maurice. 2004. 'Addams's Radical Democracy: Moving Beyond Rights'. *The Journal of Speculative Philosophy*, 18 (3): 316–223.
Haraway, Donna. 2006. 'Encounters with Companion Species: Entangling Dogs, Baboons, Philosophers and Biologists'. *Configurations*, 14 (1–2): 97–114.

Haug, Jutta. 2001. 'More Fairness, Democracy and Transparency'. *Intereconomics*, 36 (5): 226–228.
Hay, Colin. 2007. *Why We Hate Politics*. Cambridge, UK: Polity Press.
Head, Randolph C. 1995. *Early Modern Democracy in the Grisons: Social Order and Political Language in a Swiss Mountain Canton, 1470–1620*. New York: Cambridge University Press.
Held, David. 2006. *Models of Democracy*. 3rd edn. London: Polity Press.
Helfman, Gene S. 1984. 'School Fidelity in Fishes: The Yellow Perch Pattern'. *Animal Behaviour*, 32 (3): 663–672.
Herodotus. 1996 [460 BCE]. *Histories*. Translated by G. Rawlinson. London: Wordsworth Classics.
Holzhaider, J. C., M. D. Sibley, A. H. Taylor, P. J. Singh, R. D. Gray and G. R. Hunt. 2011. 'The Social Structure of New Caledonian Crows'. *Animal Behavior*, 81 (1): 83–92.
Hook, Sidney. 1949. 'The Philosophy of Democracy as a Philosophy of History'. *Philosophy and Phenomenological Research*, 9 (3): 576–587.
Huntington, Samuel. 1991. *The Third Wave: Democratization in the Late Twentieth Century*. Norman, OK, USA: University of Oklahoma Press.
Ikeskamp, Karl-J. and Henry Heitmann-Gordon. 2010. *Reconstructing the Roman Republic*. Princeton, NJ: Princeton University Press.
Insua, David Rios and Simon French (eds) 2010. *E-Democracy: A Group Decision and Negotiation Perspective*. International: Springer.
Isakhan, Benjamin and Stephen Stockwell. 2011. *Secret History of Democracy*. Basingstoke, UK: Palgrave Macmillan.
Isakhan, Benjamin. 2012. *Democracy in Iraq*. Farnham, UK: Ashgate.
Isakhan, Benjamin. 2012a. 'The Complex and Contested History of Democracy'. In Benjamin Isakhan and Stephen Stockwell *The Edinburgh Companion to the History of Democracy*. Edinburgh, UK: Edinburgh University Press, pp. 1–26.
Isakhan, Benjamin and Stephen Stockwell (eds) 2012. *The Edinburgh Companion to the History of Democracy*. Edinburgh, UK: Edinburgh University Press.
Isakhan, Benjamin and Jean-Paul Gagnon. 2013. 'Discussing the History of Democracy'. *Journal of Democratic Theory* [Forthcoming].
Itoh, Masaya, Hideki Takahashi, Takeshi Fujii, Hideyuki Takakura, Yoshihiro Hamakawa and Yasuhiro Matsumoto. 2001. 'Evaluation of Electric Energy Performance by Democratic Module pv System Field Test'. *Solar Energy Materials and Solar Cells*, 67 (1–4): 435–440.

Izawa, Ei-Ichi. 2007. 'Cognitive Basis of Social Behaviour in the Crow: Understanding "Who" Is Doing "What"'. *Neuroscience Research,* 58 (1): S17.

Izawa, Ei-Ichi. 2008. 'Crows Are "Feathered Primates"?: from Ecology to Social Cognition of Crows'. *Comparative Biochemistry and Physiology Part B: Biochemistry and Molecular Biology,* 151 (4): 445.

Jennissen, Roel. 2011. 'Ethnic Migration in Central and Eastern Europe: Its Historical Background and Contemporary Flows'. *Studies in Ethnicity and Nationalism,* 11 (2): 252–270.

Jones, Philip James. 1997. *The Italian City-State: From Commune to Signoria.* Oxford, UK: Clarendon Press.

Kacser, H. and J. A. Burns. 1979. 'Molecular Democracy: Who Shares the Controls?' *Biochemical Society Transactions,* 7 (5): 1149–1160.

Karl, G. and J. J. Simpson. 2002. 'Are Neutrinos Democratic?' *High Energy Physics – Phenomenology.* Online source: http://arxiv.org/ftp/hep-ph/papers/0205/0205288.pdf. Last accessed 12/12/2012.

Karsai, Istvan and John W. Wenzel. 2000. 'Organization and Regulation of Nest Construction Behavior in Metapolybia Wasps'. *Journal of Insect Behavior,* 13 (1): 111–140.

Kaupp, Ulrich Benjamin, Nachiket D. Kashikar and Ingo Weyand. 2008. 'Mechanisms of Sperm Chemotaxis'. *Annual Review of Physiology,* 70: 93–117.

Keane, John. 2009. *The Life and Death of Democracy.* New York: Simon and Schuster.

Keane, John. 2012a. 'By the People'. *Financial Times,* 14 December. Online source: http://www.ft.com/intl/cms/s/2/adfc52a6-438f-11e2-a48c-00144feabdco.html#axzz2R4braDBv. Last visited 21/04/2013.

Keane, John and Jean-Paul Gagnon. 2013. 'Broadening theDemocratic Imagination'. In Jean-Paul Gagnon *Democratic Theorists in Conversation: Turns in Contemporary Thought.* Basingstoke, UK: Palgrave Macmillan.

Keane, John. 2013a. 'The Greening of Democracy'. *The Conversation,* 5 September. Online source: https://theconversation.edu.au/the-greening-of-democracy-7182. Last accessed 12/12/2012.

Kendal, Jeremy R., Luke Rendell, Thomas W. Pike and Kevin L. Laland. 2008. 'Nine-Spined Sticklebacks Deploy a Hill-Climbing Social Learning Strategy'. *Behavioral Ecology,* 20 (2): 238–244.

Khatab, Sayed and Gary D. Bouma. 2007. *Democracy in Islam.* London: Routledge.

King, Andrew J. and Cédric Sueur. 2011. 'Where Next? Group Coordination and Collective Decision Making by Primates'. *International Journal of Primatology*, 32: 1245–1267.

Koide, Yoshio and Hideo Fusaoka. 2002. 'A Unified Description of Quark and Lepton Mass Matrices in a Universal Seesaw Model'. *High Energy Physics – Phenomenology*. Online source: http://arxiv.org/pdf/hep-ph/0209148v1.pdf. Last accessed 12/12/2012.

Korb, Judith. 2008. 'The Ecology of Social Evolution in Termites'. In Judith Korb and J. Heinze *Ecology of Social Evolution*. Berlin: Springer-Verlag, pp. 151–174.

Kornblith, Miriam. Translated by Vinay Jawahar. 2005. 'Elections versus Democracy'. *Journal of Democracy*, 16 (1): 124–137.

Kropotkin, Pyotr Alexeyevich. 1955 [1902]. *Mutual Aid: A Factor of Evolution*. Boston, MA: Extending Horizons.

Kroyter, Michael. 2011. 'Democratic Superstring Field Theory: Gauge Fixing'. *Journal of High Energy Physics – Theory*. 2nd updated draft. Online source: http://arxiv.org/pdf/1010.1662v4.pdf. Last accessed 12/12/2012.

Labutina, T.L. [Лабутина, ТЛ]. 1994. 'У истоков современной демократии: политическая мысль английского просвещения, 1689–1714 гг [At the Root of Modern Democracy: Political Thought in English Education, 1689–1714]'. Российская академия наук [Russian Academy of Sciences].

Laclau, Ernesto. 2001. 'Democracy and the Question of Power'. *Constellations*, 8 (1): 3–14.

Lake, Celinda and Jennifer Sosin. 1998. 'Public Opinion Polling and the Future of Democracy'. *National Civic Review*, 87 (1): 65–71.

Latour, Bruno. 1994. 'Pragmatogonies: A Mythical Account of How Humans and Nonhumans Swap Properties'. *The American Behavioural Scientist*, 37 (6): 791–809.

Levy, Ron. 2010. 'Breaking the Constitutional Deadlock: Lessons from Deliberative Experiments in Constitutional Change'. *Melbourne University Law Review*, 34: 805–838.

Lewis, I. M. 1999 [first edition 1961]. *A Pastoral Democracy: a Study of Pastoralism and Politics Among the Northern Somali of the Horn of Africa*, 3rd edn. Oxford, UK: James Currey, with the International African Anthropology Series.

Lihoreau, M., J. T. Costa and C. Rivault. 2012. 'The Social Biology of Domiciliary Cockroaches: Colony Structure, Kin Recognition and Collective Decisions'. *Insectes Sociaux* [Social Insects], 59 (4): 445–452.

DOI: 10.1057/9781137338662

Lijphart, Arend. 2001. 'Democracy in the 21st Century: Can We Be Optimistic?' *European Review*, 9 (2): 169–184.

Magalhães, Fernando. 2000. 'O passado ameaça o futuro: Tocqueville e a perspectiva de democracia individualista [The Past Threatens the Future: Tocqueville and the Prospect of Individualistic Democracy]'. *Tempo Social* [Social Time], 12 (1): 141–161.

Mallon, E. B., S. C. Pratt and N. R. Franks. 2001. 'Individual and Aggregated Decision Making during Nest Site Selection by the Ant *Leptothorax albipennis*'. *Behavioural Ecology and Sociobiology*, 50: 352–359.

Manassa, R. P. and M. I. McCormick. 2012. 'Social Learning and Acquired Recognition of a Predator by a Marine Fish'. *Animal Cognition*, 15 (4): 559–565.

Maransky, B. P. and K. L. Bildstein. 2001. 'Follow Your Elders: Age-Related Differences in the Migration Behaviour of Broad-Winged Hawks at Hawk Mountain Sanctuary, Pennsylvania'. *The Wilson Bulletin*, 113: 350–353.

Marktanner, Marcus and Joanna Nasr. 2009. 'Potentials of Democratization, Demilitarization, Industrialization, and Contraception'. *Journal of Economic Studies*, 36 (3): 236–249.

McDowell, A. 1999. *Village Life in Ancient Egypt: Laundry Lists and Love Songs*. Oxford, UK: Oxford University Press.

McGowan, Hamish, Samuel Marx, Patrick Moss and Andrew Hammond. 2012. 'Evidence of ENSO Mega-Drought Triggered Collapse of Prehistory Aboriginal Society in Northwest Australia'. *Geophyiscal Research Letters*, 39.

Mech, L. D. and L. Boitani (eds) 2003. *Wolves: Behavior, Ecology and Conservation*. Chicago: University of Chicago Press.

Meierhenrich, Uwe. 2008. *Amino Acids and the Asymmetry of Life: Caught in the Act of Formation*. International: Springer.

Mellor, Ronald. 2010. *Tacitus' Annals*. Oxford, UK: Oxford University Press.

Memel-Fotê, Harris. 1991. 'Des ancêtres fondateurs aux Pères de la nation. Introduction à une anthropologie de la démocratie' [The Founding Ancestors of the Fathers of the Nation. Introduction to the Anthropology of Democracy]. *Cahiers d'Études Africaines [Notebooks of African Studies]*, 31 (123): 263–285.

Meskell, L. 1998. 'An Archaeology of Social Relations in an Egyptian Village'. *Journal of Archaeological Method and Theory*, 5 (3): 209–243.

DOI: 10.1057/9781137338662

Mitchell-Boyask, Robin. 2009. 'Plague and Theatre in Ancient Athens'. *The Lancet*, 373 (9661): 374–375.

Milius, Susan. 2006. 'Naked and Not: Two Species of Mole Rats Run Complex Societies Underground'. *Science News*, 169 (25): 394–396.

Millar, Fergus. 1998. *The Crowd in Rome in the late Republic*. Ann Arbor, MI: University of Michigan Press.

Miura, Takahiro, Eiichi Takasugi and Masaki Yoshimura. 2000. 'Quantum Effects for the Neutrino Mixing Matrix in a Democratic Type Model'. *Progress of Theoretical Physics*, 104 (6): 1173–1187.

Mouffe, Chantal. 1999. 'Deliberative Democracy Or Agonistic Pluralism?' *Social Research*, 66 (3): 745–758.

Muhlberger, Steve. 2011. 'Republics and Quasi-Democratic Institutions in Ancient India'. In Benjamin Isakhan and Stephen Stockwell's *The Secret History of Democracy*. Basingstoke, UK: Palgrave Macmillan.

Nagy, Maté, Zsuzsa Akos, Dora Biro and Tamas Vicsek. 2010. 'Hierarchical Group Dynamics in Pigeon Flocks'. *Nature*, 464 (893): 890–893.

Nakagaki, Toshiyuki. 2001. 'Smart Behaviour of True Slime Mould in a Labyrinth'. *Research in Microbiology*, 152 (9): 767–770.

Nishikawa, Koji, Hidenori Kawamura and Azuma Ohuchi. 2005. 'Entropy and Mutual Information Analysis of Collective Behavior in Slime Mold Model'. *Advances in Soft Computing*, 29: 316–323.

Oberholzer, Michael, Miguel A. Lopez, Bryce T. McLelland and Kent L. Hill. 2010. 'Social Motility in African Trypanosomes'. *PLOS Pathogens*, 6 (1): 1–8.

O'Neill, Daniel I. 2007. 'John Adams versus Mary Wollstonecraft on the French Revolution and Democracy'. *Journal of the History of Ideas*, 68 (3): 451–476.

Paine, Phil and Steve Muhlberger. 1993. 'Democracy's Place in World History'. *Journal of World History*, 4 (1): 23–45.

Papanikolaou, Aristotle. 2003. 'Byzantium, Orthodoxy, and Democracy'. *Journal of the American Academy of Religion*, 71 (1): 75–98.

Parpola, S. 2000. 'The Mesopotamian Soul of Western Culture'. *Bulletin of the Canadian Society for Mesopotamian Studies*, 35: 29–34.

Pateman, Carole. 2012. 'Participatory Democracy Revisited'. *Perspectives on Politics*, 10 (1): 7–19.

Pezzaglia, William M. 1999. 'Dimensionally Democratic Calculus and Principles of Polydimensional Physics'. *Proceedings of the 5th*

International Conference on Clifford Algebras and their Applications in Mathematical Physics, Ixtapa-Zihuatanejo, 27 June– 4 July.
Prins, H. H. T. 1996. *Ecology and Behaviour of the African Buffalo: Social Inequality and Decision Making.* London: Chapman and Hall.
Pritchard, David. 2010. *War, Democracy, and Culture in Classical Athens.* Cambridge, UK: Cambridge University Press.
Pross, Addy. 2011. 'Toward a General Theory of Evolution: Extending Darwinian Theory to Inanimate Matter'. *Journal of Systems Chemistry,* 2 (1): 1–14.
Rador, Tonguç. 2005. 'Vibrating Winding Branes, Wrapping Democracy and Stabilization of Extra Dimensions in Dilaton Gravity'. *Journal of High Energy Physics,* 6: 1–11.
Raflaub, Kurt A., Josiah Ober and Robert Wallace. 2007. *Origins of Democracy in Ancient Greece.* Los Angeles: University of California Press.
Randerson, James. 2003. 'Together We Are Stronger'. *New Scientist,* 177 (2386): S1.
Rapeli, Lauri. 2012. 'What Should the Citizen Know About Politics? Two Approaches to the Measurement of Political Knowledge'. *Journal of Democratic Theory* [forthcoming].
Rapeli, Lauri. 2013. *The Conception of Citizen Knowledge in Democratic Theory.* Basingstoke, UK: Palgrave Macmillan [forthcoming].
Raveling, D. G. 1969. 'Preflight and Flight Behavior of Canada Geese'. *The Auk,* 86: 671–681.
Reader, S. M., J. R. Kendal and K. N. Laland. 2003. 'Social Learning of Foraging Sites and Escape Routes in Wild Trinidadian Guppies'. *Animal Behaviour,* 66: 729–739.
Reichardt, Rolf. 1994. '"Im namen der Frankenrepublik" aux origines d'une culture démocratique en Allemagne ["In the Name of the Republic of France": the Origins of a Democratic Culture in Germany]'. *Annales historiques de la Révolution française* [Historical Annals of the French Revolution], 66 (296): 235–255.
Reinhardt, V., A. Reinhardt and D. Houser. 1987. 'Prompted Progression Order in a Troop of Captive Rhesus-Monkeys'. *Folia Primatologica,* 48: 121–124.
Rendell, Luke and Hal Whitehead. 2001. 'Culture in Whales and Dolphins'. *Behavioral and Brain Sciences,* 24 (2): 309–324.
Reuven, Peter and Avigdor Eldar. 2011. 'Macromotives and Microbehaviors: the Social Dimension of Bacterial Phenotypic Variability'. *Current Opinion in Genetics & Development,* 21 (6): 759–767.

DOI: 10.1057/9781137338662

Roach, Kate. 2011. 'Let's Stick Together'. *New Scientist*, 211 (2830): 52–55.
Robinson, Donald L. 2011. *Town Meeting: Practicing Democracy in Rural New England.* Boston, MA: University of Massachusetts Press.
Roe, Bjorn. 2002. 'The Good, the Bad and the Evil Athens: Quality of Life in Cities'. *Ekistics*, 69 (412–414): 123–130.
Rosati, Alexandra G. and Brian Hare. 2012. 'Decision Making across Social Contexts: Competition Increases Preferences for Risk in Chimpanzees and Bonobos'. *Animal Behaviour*, 84 (4): 869–879.
Rumsey, Clifton C. and L. F. Abbott. 2006. 'Synaptic Democracy in Active Dendrites'. *Journal of Neurophysiology*, 96 (5): 2307–2318.
Russell, Eleanor and Ian Rowley. 2000. 'Demography and Social Organization of the Red-Winged Fairy-Wren, *Malurus elegans*'. *Australian Journal of Zoology*, 48 (2): 161–200.
Ryder, Thomas B., David B. McDonald, John G. Blake, Patricia G. Parker and Bette A. Loiselle. 2008. 'Social Networks in the Lek-Mating Wire-Tailed Manakin (*Pipra filicauda*)'. *Proceedings of the Royal Society B – Biological Sciences*, 275 (1641): 1367–1374.
Sader, Emir. 2010. 'Vivir la revolución [Living the Revolution]'. *Revista Internacional de Filosofia Iberoamericana y Teoria Social* [International Latin American Review of Philosophy and Social Theory]. 15 (43): 97–100.
Sakai, Mai, Ding Wang, Kexiong Wang, Songhai Li and Tomonari Akamatsu. 2011. 'Do Porpoises Choose Their Associates? A New Method for Analyzing Social Relationships among Cetaceans'. *PLOS One*, 6 (12): 1–8.
Sakakura, Yoshitaka and Katsumi Tsukamoto. 1999. 'Ontogeny of Aggressive Behaviour in Schools of Yellowtail, Seriola Quinqueradiata'. *Environmental Biology of Fishes*, 56 (1–2): 231–242.
Saward, Michael. 2003. *Democracy*. Cambridge, UK: Polity Press.
Saward, Michael (ed.) 2006. *Democracy.* London: Routledge.
Schärer, Lukas, D. Timothy J. Littlewood, Andrea Waeschenbach, Wataru Yoshida and Dita B. Vizoso. 2011. 'Mating Behavior and the Evolution of Sperm Design'. *Proceedings of the National Academy of Science USA*, 108 (4): 1490–1495.
Schemeil, Yves. 2000. 'Democracy before Democracy?' *International Political Science Review*, 21 (2): 99–120.
Schwartz, Christine Patrice. 2010. 'Neurobiology of Bat Vocal Behavior'. Doctoral Dissertation. Texas A&M University, USA.

Seeley, Thomas. 2011. *Honeybee Democracy*. Princeton, NJ: Princeton University Press.

Seeley, Thomas and Jean-Paul Gagnon. 2013. 'Nonhuman Democratic Practice'. In Jean-Paul Gagnon *Democratic Theorists in Conversation: Turns in Contemporary Thought*. Basingstoke, UK: Palgrave Macmillan.

Selg, Peeter. 2012. 'Justice and Liberal Strategy: Towards a Radical Democratic Reading of Rawls'. *Social Theory and Practice*, 38 (1): 83–114.

Segre, Gavriel. 2010. 'Quantum Democracy Is Possible'. Version two of a working paper. Online source: http://arxiv.org/pdf/0806.3667v4.pdf. Last accessed 12/12/2012.

Sissa, Giulia. 2012. 'Democracy: A Persian Invention?' *Mètis: Anthropologie des mondes grecs anciens*, 10: 227–261.

Smukalla, Scott, Marina Caldara, Nathalie Pochet, Anne Beauvais, Stephanie Guadagnini, Chen Yan, Marcelo D. Vinces, An Jansen, Marie Christine Prevost, Jean-Paul Latgé, Gerald R. Fink, Kevin R. Foster and Kevin J. Verstreppen. 2008. '*FLO1* Is a Variable Green Beard Gene that Drives Biofilm-like Cooperation in Budding Yeast'. *Cell*, 135 (4): 726–737.

Sterratt, David C. and Arjen van Ooyen. 2004. 'Does a Dendritic Democracy Need a Ruler?' *Neurocomputing*, 58–60: 437–442.

Stockwell, Stephen. 2011. 'Engaging Secret Democracy Before and After Athens'. *Journal of Democratic Theory*, 2 (1).

Sultansoy, Saleh. 2006. 'Flavor Democracy in Particle Physics'. *Invited Presentation at the Sixth International Conference of the Balkan Physical Union*, August 22–26, Istanbul, Turkey.

Tebes, Juan Manuel. 2007. 'Assyrians, Judeans, Pastoral Groups, and the Trade Patterns in the Late Iron Age Negev'. *History Compass*, 5 (2): 619–631.

Thomas, Gordon K. 1990. 'Common Dawn? Wordsworth and the Philosophy of Democracy'. *Neophilologus*, 74 (2): 310–317.

Tilly, Charles. 2007. *Democracy*. Cambridge, UK: Cambridge University Press.

Tóth, Zoltán, Veronika Bókony, Ádám Z. Lendvai, Krisztián Szabó, Zsolt Pénzes and András Liker. 2009. 'Whom Do the Sparrows Follow? the Effect of Kinship on Social Preference in House Sparrow Flocks'. *Behavioural Processes*, 82 (2): 173–177.

DOI: 10.1057/9781137338662

Tribe, Laurence H. 1989. 'The Curvature of Constitutional Space: What Lawyers Can Learn From Modern Physics'. *Harvard Law Review*, 103 (1): 1–39.

Ugarte, Ignacio Cremades. 2009. 'La contrautopía nacionalista de Baroja, la República del Bidasoa [The Nationalistic Contra-Utopia of Baroja, the Republic of the Bidasoa]'. *Cuadernos de Historia del Derecho* [Notebooks on the History of Law], 16: 7–35.

Urbinati, Nadia. 2010. 'Unpolitical Democracy'. *Political Theory*, 38 (1): 65–92.

Urry, John. 2006. 'Complexity'. *Theory, Culture and Society*, 23 (2–3): 111–115.

Villareal, Luis P. 2009. *Origin of Group Identity: Viruses, Addiction and Cooperation.* International: Springer.

Waal, Frans B. M. de. 1995. 'Bonobo Sex and Society: the Behaviour of a Close Relative Challenges Assumptions about Male Supremacy in Human Evolution'. *Scientific American*, 272 (3): 82–88.

Waal, Frans B. M. de. 1997. 'Bonobo Dialogues'. *Natural History*, 106 (4): 22–25.

Waddell, David R. and Günter Vogel. 1985. 'Phagocytic Behaviour Or the Predatory Slime Mould, *Dictyostelium caveatum:* Cell Nibbling'. *Experimental Cell Research*, 159 (2): 323–334.

Wollstonecraft, Mary. 1795. *An Historical and Moral View of the French Revolution; and the Effect it Has Produced in Europe.* London, UK: Printed for J. Johnson in St. Paul's Churchyard.

Ward, Michael P. and Arlo Raim. 2011. 'The Fly-and-Social Foraging Hypothesis for Diurnal Migration: Why American Crows Migrate during the Day'. *Behavioural Ecology and Social Biology*, 65 (7): 1411–1418.

Wascher, Claudia A. F., Georgine Szipl, Markus Boeckle and Anna Wilkinson. 2012. 'You Sound Familiar: Carrion Crows Can Differentiate between the Calls of Known and Unknown Heterospecifics'. *Animal Cognition*, 15 (5): 1015–1019.

Weale, Albert. 2007. *Democracy*. 2nd edn. Basingstoke, UK: Palgrave Macmillan.

Weale, Albert and Jean-Paul Gagnon. 2013. 'The Changing History of Democracy'. In Jean-Paul Gagnon *Democratic Theorists in Conversation: Turns in Contemporary Thought.* Basingstok, UK: Palgrave Macmillan.

DOI: 10.1057/9781137338662

Weitman, Sasha Reinhard. 1968. 'Bureaucracy, Democracy and the French Revolution'. PhD Thesis. Washington University, USA.

Welch, G. Rickey and Tamás Keleti. 1987. 'Is Cell Metabolism Controlled by a "Molecular Democracy" or by a "Supramolecular Socialism"?' *Trends in Biochemical Sciences,* 12: 216–217.

Whitman, John. 2010. 'Brother Sperm Train Together'. *Nature.com.* Online source: http://www.nature.com/news/2010/100120/full/news.2010.22.html. Last accessed: 20/12/2012.

Wingenbach, Ed. 2011. *Institutionalizing Agonistic Democracy: Post-Foundationalism and Political Liberalism.* Farnham, UK: Ashgate.

Woese, C. 1998. 'The Universal Ancestor'. *Proceedings of the National Academy of Science USA,* 95: 6854–6859.

Wood, Gordon. 1969. *The Creation of the American Republic 1776–1787.* New York: Norton Press.

Wright, Quincy. 1949. 'Philosophical Inquiry into Current Ideological Conflicts: The Meaning of Democracy'. *United Nations Educational, Scientific and Cultural Organization.* Paris, 10 March.

Würsig, Bernd. 1988. 'The Behavior of Baleen Whales'. *Scientific American,* 258 (4): 102–107.

Yao, Yurong and Lisa Murphy. 2007. 'Remote Electronic Voting Systems: An Exploration of Voters' Perceptions and Intention to Use'. *European Journal of Information Systems,* 16 (2): 106–120.

Yosida, Shigeto and Kazuo Okanoya. 2009. 'Naked Mole-Rat is Sensitive to Social Hierarchy Encoded in Antiphonal Vocalization'. *Ethology,* 115 (9): 823–831.

Young, Iris Marion. 2002. *Inclusion and Democracy.* Oxford, UK: Oxford University Press.

DOI: 10.1057/9781137338662

Index

 DOI: 10.1057/9781137338662

DOI: 10.1057/9781137338662

Lightning Source UK Ltd.
Milton Keynes UK
UKOW04n0600110214

226255UK00002B/23/P

9 781137 338655